D0788648

RISKS OF FAITH

ALSO BY JAMES H. CONE

Speaking the Truth: Ecumenism, Liberation,
and Black Theology

God of the Oppressed

Black Theology and Black Power

Martin & Malcolm & America:
A Dream or a Nightmare

The Spirituals and the Blues:
An Interpretation

A Black Theology of Liberation

My Soul Looks Back

For My People: Black Theology
and the Black Church

Risks of Faith

James H. Cone

THE EMERGENCE OF

A BLACK THEOLOGY

OF LIBERATION, 1968–1998

BOSTON   *Beacon Press*

Beacon Press
25 Beacon Street
Boston, Massachusetts *02108-2892*
www.beacon.org

Beacon Press books
are published under the auspices of the
Unitarian Universalist Association of Congregations.

© 1999 by James H. Cone
All rights reserved
Printed in the United States of America

05 04 03 02 01 00 99   8 7 6 5 4 3 2 1

Text design by Wesley B. Tanner/Passim Editions
Composition by Wilsted & Taylor Publishing Services

Library of Congress Cataloging-in-Publication Data

Cone, James H.
    Risks of faith : the emergence of a Black theology of liberation,
    1968–1998 / James H. Cone.
        p.   cm.
    Includes bibliographical references and index.
    ISBN 0-8070-0950-4 (cloth)
    1. Black theology.   2. Black power.   I. Title.
BT82.7.C675   1999
230'.089'96073—dc21   99-28327

FOR GAYRAUD S. WILMORE

My friend and colleague in the black theology movement,
who was never afraid to take risks for black people

*And for communities of color throughout the world,
for whom risks of faith are a daily reality*

Contents

Introduction
Looking Back, Going Forward

This book provides an opportunity for me to reflect on the origin and development of my theological perspective. When I think about my vocation, I go back to my childhood years in Bearden, Arkansas—a rural community of approximately 1,200 people. I do not remember Bearden for nostalgic reasons. In fact, I seldom return there in person, because of persistent racial tensions in my relations to the whites and lingering ambivalence in my feelings toward the blacks. I am not and do not wish to be Bearden's favorite son. My brother, Cecil, also a theologian and a preacher, has been bestowed that honor by the African-American community, a distinction he gladly accepts and a role he fulfills quite well.

I remember Bearden because it is the place where I first discovered myself—as *black* and *Christian*. There, the meaning of black was defined primarily by the menacing presence of whites, which no African-American could escape. I grew up during the age of Jim Crow (1940s and early '50s). I attended segregated schools, drank water from "colored" fountains, saw movies from balconies, and when absolutely necessary greeted white adults at the back doors of their homes. I also observed the contempt and brutality that white law meted out to the blacks who transgressed their racial mores or who dared to question their authority. Bearden white people, like most Southerners of that time, could be mean and vicious, and I, along with other blacks, avoided them whenever possible as if they were poisonous snakes.

The Christian part of my identity was shaped primarily at Macedonia A.M.E. Church. Every Sunday and sometimes on weeknights I encountered Jesus through rousing sermons, fervent prayers, spirited gospel songs, and the passionate testimonies of the people. Jesus was the dominant reality at Macedonia and in black life in Bearden. The people walked with him and told him about their troubles as if he were a trusted friend who understood their trials and tribulations in this unfriendly world. They called Jesus "the lily of the valley and the bright and morning star," the "Rose of Sharon and the Lord of life," a "very present help in time of trouble." The people often shouted and danced, clapped their hands and stamped their feet as they bore witness to the power of Jesus' Spirit in their midst—"building them up where they are torn down and propping them up on every leaning side."

Like the people of Macedonia, Jesus became a significant presence in my life, too. I do not remember the exact date or time I "turned to Jesus," as the conversion experience was called. At home, church, and school, at play and at work, Jesus was always there, as the anchor of life, giving it meaning and purpose and bestowing hope and faith in the ultimate justice of things. Jesus was that reality who empowered black people to know that they were not the worthless human beings that white people said they were.

There were no atheists in "Cotton Belt," as the "colored" section of Bearden was called—no proclaimers of Nietzsche's "God is dead" philosophy and none of the "cultured despisers" of religion that Friedrich Schleiermacher wrote to in 1799. The closest to Nietzsche's atheists and Schleiermacher's "cultured despisers" were the bluespeople who drank corn whiskey and boogied slowly and sensually to the deep guttural sound of the raunchy music at the jook joints every Friday and Saturday night. The sounds of Bessie Smith, Muddy Waters, and Howlin' Wolf took center-stage as they belted out the lowdown dirty blues in songs like "I Used to Be Your Sweet Mama," "Hoochie Coochie Man," and "Somebody in My Home."

Unlike the churchpeople, the bluespeople found the Sunday religion of Jesus inadequate for coping with their personal problems and the social contradictions they experienced during the week. As churchpeople soothed their souls with the song "Lord, I Want to Be a Christian in My Heart," the people at the honky-tonk transcended their agony by facing it with stoic defiance or, as James Baldwin called it, "ironic tenacity"[1]: "I got the blues, but I'm too damned mean to cry."

Sometimes sharp tensions emerged between the celebrants of Saturday night and those of Sunday morning. But each group respected the other, because both knew that they were seeking, each in its own way, to cope with the same troubles of life. Some people moved between the two groups during different periods of their lives, as my father did. But it was not possible to be a member in good standing in both groups at the same time, because the church demanded that an individual make a choice between the blues and the spirituals, between the "devil's music" and the "sweet melodies of Jesus." Baptist and Methodist churches, the only black denominations in Bearden, regularly accepted backsliders back into the fold, provided they repented of their wrongdoing and declared their intentions to lead good and righteous lives in service to the Lord. My father had a few lapses in faith, because he found it hard to cope with life's adversities without taking a nip of gin and hanging out with the bluespeople in order to add a little spice to life not found at the church. But my mother monitored him closely, and Macedonia readily received him back into the community of the faithful as often as he publicly repented.

What puzzled me most during my childhood about the religion of Jesus were not the tensions between Saturday night and Sunday morning in black life but rather the conspicuous presence of the color bar in white churches. In Bearden, like the rest of America, Sunday was the most segregated day of the week. Black and white Christians had virtually no social or religious dealings with each other, even though both were Baptists and Methodists—reading the same Bible, worshiping the same God, and reciting the same confessions of faith in their congregations.

Although whites posted "Welcome" signs outside their churches, ostensibly beckoning all visitors to join them in worship, blacks knew that the invitation did not include them. "What kind of Christianity is it that preaches love and practices segregation?" my brother Cecil and I, budding young theologians, often asked each other. "How could whites exclude black people from their churches and still claim Jesus as their Savior and the Bible as their holy book?" We talked about testing the theological integrity of white faith by seeking to integrate one of their churches, but felt that the risks of bodily harm were too great.

Despite the ever present reality of white supremacy, I do not ever remember experiencing a feeling of inferiority because of what whites said about me or about other black people. One reason was the stellar example my father and mother set for me. They were part of that cloud of black witnesses that James Baldwin wrote about who "in the teeth of the most terrible odds, achieved an unassailable and monumental dignity."[2] They taught me what Baldwin told his nephew: "You can only be destroyed by believing that you really are what the white world calls a *nigger*."[3]

My parents were strong and self-confident—exhibiting a determined opposition to white supremacy and creative leadership and great courage when they and the black community faced adversity. Charlie and Lucy, as the people in Bearden called them, were immensely intelligent, even though they had little opportunity for formal education, having completed only the sixth and ninth grades, respectively. (With the support and encouragement of my father, my mother went back and completed high school where her sons had graduated earlier and also went on to finish her college degree four years later. She then returned to teach in Bearden. I was struck by her determination.) Their education, they often told their sons, came from the "school of hard knocks"—the experience of surviving with dignity in a society that did not recognize black humanity.

The faith of Macedonia, which my parents imbibed deeply, was a powerful antidote against the belief that blacks were less than whites. According to this faith, God created all people equal—as brothers and sisters in the church and the society. No person or group is better than any other. As evidence for that claim, preachers and teachers often cited the text from the prophet Malachi: "Have we not all one father? Hath not one God created us?" (2:10 Authorized [King James] Version). They also quoted Paul, *selectively*—carefully avoiding the ambiguous and problematic texts, especially in *Philemon* where Paul returned the slave Onesimus to his master and in *Ephesians* where servants were told to "be obedient to them who are your masters . . . as unto Christ" (Eph. 6:5 AV).

Preachers and Sunday School teachers at Macedonia were quite skilled in picking biblical texts that affirmed their humanity. They especially liked Luke's account of Paul's sermon on Mars' Hill where he said God "made of one blood all nations of men [and women] to dwell on the face of the earth" (Acts 17:26 AV). They also quoted Paul's letter to the Galatians: "There is neither Jew nor Greek . . . neither slave nor free . . . neither male nor female." We are "all one in Christ Jesus" (3:28 AV)—blacks and whites, as well as other human colors and orientations. When one truly believes that gospel and internalizes it in one's way of life, as I and many black Christians in Bearden did, it is possible to know that "you are somebody" even though the world treats you like nobody.

From the time I was conscious of being black and Christian, I recognized that I was a problem for America's white politicians and invisible to most of its practitioners of religion. I did not quite understand what made me a problem or invisible since skin color appeared to be a minor difference between human beings. Yet politicians found it difficult to pass laws to protect black humanity. Even those passed were rarely enforced. White ministers seemed not to notice the daily white assault on black humanity. They preached sermons about loving God and thy neighbor as if the violence that whites committed against blacks did not invalidate their Christian identity.

While struggling to understand how whites reconciled racism with their Christian identity, I also encountered an uncritical faith in many black churches. Blacks not only seemed to tolerate anti-intellectualism as whites tolerated racism; but, like most whites in relation to racism, often promoted it. It was as if the less one knew and the louder one shouted Jesus' name, the closer one was to God.

I found it hard to believe that the God of Jesus condoned ignorance as if it were a virtue. It contradicted what my parents and teachers taught me about the value of education and a disciplined mind. It also contradicted what I read in history books about black slaves who risked life and limb in order to learn to read and write so they could understand more clearly the meaning of the freedom to which God had called them. I was, therefore, deeply troubled by the anti-intellectualism that permeated many aspects of the ministry in the Black Church.

How could ministers preach the gospel in a world they did not understand? How can they understand the gospel without disciplined reflections and critical debate? "A religion that won't stand the application of reason and common sense," wrote W. E. B. Du Bois, "is not fit for an intelligent dog."[4]

The search for a reasoned faith in a complex and ever changing world was the chief motivation that led me to study at Garrett Theological Seminary (now Garrett-Evangelical). It seemed that the more I learned about the gospel through a critical study of the Bible, history, theology, and the practice of ministry the more I needed and wanted to know about it. I wanted to explore its meanings for different social, political, and cultural contexts, past and present.

Theology quickly became my favorite subject in seminary because it opened the door to explore faith's meaning for the current time and situation in which I was living. I loved the give-and-take of theological debate and eagerly waited for the opportunity during and after classes to engage my professors and fellow students on the burning theological issues of the day. That was why I remained at Garrett and Northwestern University for the Ph.D. in systematic theology. While writing a dissertation on Karl

Barth's anthropology, I thought I had enough knowledge of the Christian faith to communicate it to persons anywhere in the world. Who would not feel adequately endowed after plowing through twelve volumes of Barth's *Church Dogmatics?*

In a way, my education was pulling me away from my people. The educational quest focused on mastering the theological systems of the well-known European theologians of the past and present. We students spent most of our time obediently reading books, listening to lectures, and writing papers about their views of God, Jesus, the Holy Spirit, and the church.

The Civil Rights movement of the 1960s awakened me from my theological slumber. As I became actively involved in the black freedom movement that was exploding in the streets all over America, I soon discovered how limited my seminary education was. The curriculum at Garrett and Northwestern did not deal with the questions black people were asking as they searched for the theological meaning of their fight for justice in a white racist society. And as individuals and isolated students within a demanding educational system, neither I nor the token number of black students had the intellectual resources to articulate them. I found myself grossly ill-prepared, because I knew deep down that I could not repeat to a struggling black community the doctrines of the faith as they had been reinterpreted by Barth, Bultmann, Niebuhr, and Tillich for European colonizers and white racists in the United States. I knew that before I could say anything worthwhile about God and the black situation of oppression in America I had to discover a theological identity that was accountable to the life, history, and culture of African-American people.

Recognizing the community to whom I was accountable, I wanted to know more than just what Europeans and the white Americans who emulated them thought about sacred reality. I was searching for a way to create a Christian theology out of the black experience of slavery, segregation, and the struggle for a just society. When I asked my professors about what theology had to do with the black struggle for racial justice, they seemed surprised and uncomfortable with the question, not knowing what to say, and anxious to move on with the subject matter as they understood it. I was often told that theology and the struggle for racial justice were separate subjects, with the latter belonging properly in the disciplines of sociology and political science. Although I felt a disquieting unease with that response, I did not say much about it to my professors as they skirted around talking about what the gospel had to say to black people in a white society that had defined them as nonpersons.

While reading Martin Luther King, Jr., and Malcolm X, the blackness in my theological consciousness exploded like a volcano after many dormant years. No longer able to accept black invisibility in theology and getting angrier and angrier at the white brutality meted out against Martin King and other civil rights activists, my southern, Arkansas racial identity began to rise in my theological consciousness.

"You are a racist!" I yelled angrily at my doctoral advisor who was lecturing to a theology class of about forty students. "You've been talking for weeks now about the wrongdoings of Catholics against Protestants in sixteenth and seventeenth century Europe," I continued, raising my voice even higher, "but you've said absolutely nothing about the monstrous acts of violence by *white* Protestants against Negroes in the American South *today!*"

Devastated that I—who was a frequent presence in his office and home —would call him a racist, my advisor, a grave and staid English gentleman, had no capacity for understanding black rage. He paced back and forth for nearly a minute before he stopped suddenly and stared directly at me with an aggrieved and perplexed look on his face. Then he shouted, "That's simply not true! Class dismissed."

He stormed out of the classroom to his office. I followed him. "Jim," he turned in protest, "*you* know I'm not a racist!" "I know," I said with an apologetic tone but still laced with anger. "I'm sorry I blurted out my frustrations at you. But I am angry about racism in America and the rest of the world. I find it very difficult to study theology and never talk about it in class." "I'm concerned about racism, too," he retorted with emphasis. We then talked guardedly about racism in Britain and the U.S.

The more I thought about the incident, then and later, the more I realized that my angry outburst was not about the personal prejudices of my advisor or any other professor at Garrett. It was about how the discipline of theology had been defined so as to exclude any engagement with the African-American struggle against racism. I did not have the words to say to my advisor what I deeply felt. I just knew intuitively that something was seriously wrong with studying theology during the peak of the Civil Rights era and never once reading a book about racial justice in America or talking about it in class. It was as if the black struggle for justice had nothing to do with the study of theology—a disturbing assumption, which I gradually became convinced was both anti-Christian and racist. But since I could not engage in a disinterested discussion about race as if I were analyzing Karl Barth's christology, I kept my views about racism in theology to myself and only discussed them with the small group of African-American students who had similar views.

After I completed the Ph.D. in systematic theology in the fall of 1964, I returned to Arkansas to teach at Philander Smith College in Little Rock. No longer cloistered in a white academic environment and thus free of the need of my professors' approval, I turned my attention to the rage I had repressed during six years of graduate education. Martin Luther King, Jr., and the Civil Rights movement helped me to take another look at the theological meaning of racism and the black struggle for justice. My seminary education was nearly worthless in this regard, except as a negative stimulant. My mostly neo-orthodox professors talked incessantly about the "mighty acts of God" in biblical history. But they objected to any effort to link God's righteousness with the political struggles of the poor today, especially among the black poor fighting for justice in the United States. God's righteousness, they repeatedly said, can never be identified with any human project. The secular and death-of-God theologians were not much better. They proclaimed God's death with glee and published God's obituary in *Time* magazine. But they ignored the theological significance of Martin King's proclamation of God's righteous presence in the black freedom struggle.

It is one thing to think of Martin King as a civil rights activist who transformed America's race relations and quite another to regard the struggle for racial justice as having theological significance. King was a public theologian. He turned the nations' television networks into his pulpit and classroom, and he forced white Christians to confront their own beliefs. He challenged all Americans in the church, the academy, and every segment of the culture to face head-on the great moral crisis of racism in the U.S. and the world. It was impossible to ignore King and the claims he made about religion and justice. While he never regarded himself as an academic theologian, he transformed our understanding of the Christian faith by making the practice of justice an essential ingredient of its identity.

It could be argued that Martin King's contribution to the identity of Christianity in America and the world was as far-reaching as Augustine's in the fifth century and Luther's in the sixteenth.[5] Before King, no Christian theologian showed so conclusively in his actions and words the great contradiction between racial segregation and the gospel of Jesus. In fact, racial segregation was so widely accepted in the churches and societies throughout the world that few white theologians in America and Europe regarded the practice as unjust. Those who did see the injustice did not regard the issue important enough to even write or talk about it. But after King no theologian or preacher dares to defend racial segregation. He destroyed its moral legitimacy. Even conservative white preachers like Pat Robertson and Jerry Falwell make a point to condemn racial segregation and do not want to be identified with racism. That change is due almost single-handedly to the theological power of King's actions and words.

Martin King was extremely modest about his political achievements and rather naive about the intellectual impact he made on the theological world. Theologians and seminarians also have been slow to recognize the significance of his theological contribution. But I am convinced that Martin Luther King, Jr., was the most important and influential Christian theologian in America's history. Some would argue that the honor belongs to Jonathan Edwards or Reinhold Niebuhr or even perhaps Walter Rauschenbusch. Where we come down on this issue largely depends upon how we understand the discipline of theology. Those who think that the honor belongs to Edwards or Niebuhr or Rauschenbusch regard intellect as more important than character in the doing of theology and thus do not think that the disparity between morality and intelligence affect theological insight. To place Edwards, Niebuhr, and Rauschenbusch over King means that one cannot possibly regard the achievement of racial justice as a significant theological issue, because none of them made justice for black people a central element of their theological program. Edwards, Rauschenbusch, and Niebuhr were *white* theologians who sought to speak only to their racial community. They did not use their intellectual power to support people of color in their fight for justice. Blacks and the Third World poor were virtually invisible to them.

Martin King is America's most important Christian theologian because of what he said and did about race from a theological point of view. He was a liberation theologian before the phrase was coined by African-American and Latin American religious thinkers in the late sixties and early seventies. King's mature reflections on the gospel of Jesus emerged primarily from his struggle for racial justice in America. His political practice preceded his theological reflections. He was an activist-theologian who showed that one could not be a Christian in any authentic sense without fighting for justice among people.

One can observe the priority of practice, as a hermeneutical principle, in his sermons, essays, and books. *Stride Toward Freedom* (1958), *Why We Can't Wait* (1964), and *Where Do We Go from Here?* (1967) were reflections on the political and religious meaning, respectively, of the Montgomery bus boycott (1955–56), the Birmingham movement (1963), and the rise of Black Power (1966). In these texts King defined the black freedom movement as seeking to redeem the soul of America and to liberate its political and religious institutions from the cancer of racism. I contend that as a theologian to America he surpassed the others, because he addressed our most persistent and urgent sickness.

But two other features of King's work elevate him above Edwards, Rauschenbusch, and Niebuhr. The first is his international stature and influence. I do not mean his Nobel Prize, but his contribution beyond the particularity of the Black American struggle. He influenced liberation movements in China, Ireland, Germany, India, South Africa, Korea, and the Philippines, and throughout Latin America and the Caribbean. Hardly any liberation movements among the poor are untouched by the power of his thought.

Secondly, King was North America's most courageous theologian. He did not seek the protection of a university appointment and a quiet office. One of his most famous theological statements was written in jail. Other ideas were formed in brief breathing spaces after days of exposure to physical danger in the streets of Birmingham, Selma, and Chicago and the dangerous roads of Mississippi. King did theology in solidarity with the least of these and in the face of death. "If physical death," he said, "is the price I must pay to free my white brothers and sisters from the permanent death of the spirit, then nothing could be more redemptive." Real theology is risky, as King's courageous life demonstrated.

From King black liberation theology received its Christian identity, which he understood as the practice of justice and love in human relations and the hope that God has not left the least of these alone in their suffering. However, that identity was only one factor that contributed to the creation of black liberation theology. The other was Malcolm X, who identified the struggle as a *black* struggle. As long as black freedom and the Christian way in race relations were identified exclusively with integration and nonviolence, black theology was not possible. Integration and nonviolence required blacks to turn the other cheek to white brutality, join the mainstream of American society, and do theology without anger and without reference to the history and culture of African-Americans. It meant seeing Christianity exclusively through the eyes of its white interpreters. Malcolm prevented that from happening.

Martin King helped to define my *Christian* identity but was silent about the meaning of blackness in a world of white supremacy. His public thinking about the faith was designed to persuade white Christians to take seriously the humanity of Negroes. He challenged whites to be true to what they said in their political and religious documents of freedom and democracy. What King did not initially realize was how deeply flawed white Christian thinking is regarding race and the psychological damage done to the self-image of blacks.

To understand white racism and black rage in America, I turned to Malcolm X and Black Power. While King accepted white logic, Malcolm rejected it. "When [people] get angry," Malcolm said, "they aren't interested in logic, they aren't interested in odds, they aren't interested in consequences. When they get angry, they realize that the condition that they're in—that their suffering is unjust, immoral, illegal, and that anything they do to correct it or eliminate it, they're justified. When you develop that type of anger and speak in that voice, then we'll get some kind of respect and recognition, and some changes from these people who have been promising us falsely already for far too long."[6]

Malcolm saw more clearly than King the depth and complexity of racism in America, especially in the North. The North was more clever than the South and thus knew how to camouflage its exploitation of black people. White northern liberals represented themselves as the friends of the Negro and deceived King and many other blacks into believing that they really wanted to achieve racial justice in America. But Malcolm knew better and he exposed their hypocrisy. He called white liberals "foxes" in contrast to southern "wolves." Malcolm saw no difference between the two, except that one smiles and the other growls when they eat you. Northern white liberals hated Malcolm for his uncompromising, brutal honesty. But blacks, especially the young people, loved him for it. He said publicly what most blacks felt but were afraid to say except privately among themselves.

I first heard Malcolm speak while I was a student at Garrett but I did not really listen to him. I was committed to Martin King and even hoped that he would accept the invitation offered him to become a professor of theology at Garrett. I regarded Malcolm as a racist and would have nothing to do with him. Malcolm X did not enter my theological consciousness until I left seminary and was challenged by the rise of the black consciousness movement in the middle of the 1960s. Black Power, a child of Malcolm, forced me to take a critical look at Martin King and to discover his limits.

It is one thing to recognize that the gospel of Jesus demands justice in race relations and quite another to recognize that it demands that African-Americans accept their blackness and reject its white distortions. When I turned to Malcolm, I discovered my blackness and realized that I could never be who I was called to be until I embraced my African heritage—completely and enthusiastically. He taught me that a colorless Christianity is a joke—only found in the imaginary world of white theology. It is not found in the real world of white seminaries and churches. Nor is it found in black churches. That black people hate themselves is no accident of history. As I listened to Malcolm and meditated on his analysis of racism in America and the world, I became convinced by his rhetorical virtuosity. Speaking to blacks, his primary audience, he said:

> Who taught you to hate the color of your skin? Who taught you to hate the texture of your hair? Who taught you to hate the shape of your nose? Who taught you to hate yourself from the top of your head to the sole of your feet? Who taught you to hate your own kind? Who taught you to hate the race you belong to so much that you don't want to be around each other? You should ask yourself, "Who taught you to hate being what God gave you?"[7]

Malcolm challenged me to take a critical look at Christianity, Martin King, and the Civil Rights movement. The challenge was so deep that I found myself affirming what many persons regarded as theological opposites: Martin and Malcolm, civil rights and Black Power, Christianity and blackness.

Just as Martin King may be regarded as America's most influential theologian and preacher, Malcolm X may be regarded as America's most trenchant race critic. As Martin's theological achievement may be compared to Augustine's and Luther's, Malcolm's race critique is as far-reaching as Marx's class critique and the current feminist critique of gender. Malcolm was the great master of suspicion in the area of race. No one before or after him analyzed the role of Christianity in promoting racism and its mental and material consequences upon the lives of blacks as Malcolm did. He has no peer.

Malcolm X taught black ministers and scholars that the identity of African-Americans as a people was inextricably linked with blackness. This was his great contribution to black theology. Malcolm gave black theology its *black* identity, putting blackness at the center of who we were created to be. Like Martin, Malcolm did not write a scholarly treatise on the theme of blackness and self. He revolutionized black self-understanding with the power of his speech.

The distinctiveness of black theology is the bringing together of Martin and Malcolm—their ideas about Christianity and justice and blackness and self. Neither Martin nor Malcolm sought to do that. The cultural identity of Christianity was not important to Martin because he understood it in the "universal" categories he was taught in graduate school. His main concern was to link the identity of Christianity with social justice, oriented in love and defined by hope.

The Christian identity of the black self was not important to Malcolm X. For him, Christianity was the white man's religion and thus had to be rejected. Black people, Malcolm contended, needed a black religion, one that would bestow self-respect upon them for being black. Malcolm was not interested in remaking Christianity into a black religion.

I disagreed with both Martin and Malcolm and insisted on the importance of bringing blackness and Christianity together. While Martin and Malcolm were prevented from coming together during their lifetime, I was determined to put them together in black liberation theology. Using their cultural and political insights, I discovered a way of articulating what I wanted to say about theology and race that not only rejected the need for my professors' approval, but challenged them to exorcise the racism in their theologies. Malcolm taught me how to make theology black and never again to despise my African origin. Martin showed me how to make and keep theology Christian and never allow it to be used to support injustice. I was transformed from a *Negro* theologian to a *black* theologian, from an understanding of theology as an analysis of God-ideas in books to an understanding of it as a disciplined reflection about God arising out of a commitment to the practice of justice for the poor.

The turn to blackness was an even deeper conversion-experience than the turn to Jesus. It was spiritual, transforming radically my way of seeing the world and theology. Before I was born again into thinking black, I thought of theology as something remote from my history and culture, something that was primarily defined by Europeans which I, at best, could only imitate. Blackness gave me new theological spectacles, which enabled me to move beyond the limits of white theology, and empowered my mind to think thoughts that were wild and heretical when evaluated by white academic values. Blackness opened my eyes to see African-American history and culture as one of the most insightful sources for knowing about God since the Bible was declared a canon. Blackness whetted my appetite for learning how to do theology with a black signature on it and thereby make it accountable to poor black people and not to the privileged white theological establishment. The revolution that Malcolm X created in my theological consciousness meant that I could no longer make peace with the intellectual mediocrity in which I had been trained. The more I trusted my experience the more new thoughts about God and theology whirled around in my head—so fast I could hardly contain my excitement.

Using the black experience as the starting point of theology raised the theodicy question in a profound and challenging way that was never mentioned in graduate school. It was James Baldwin's *The Fire Next Time* which poignantly defined the problem for me: "If [God's] love was so great, and if He loved all His children, why were we, the blacks, cast down so far?"[8] This was an existential, heart-wrenching question, which challenged the academic way in which the problem of evil was dealt with in graduate school. It forced me to search deep into a wellspring of blackness, not for a theoretical answer that would satisfy the dominant intellectual culture of Europe and the United States, but rather for a new way of doing theology that would empower the suffering black poor to fight for a more liberated existence.

"Christianity and Black Power" was the first essay I wrote following my black conversion. I vividly remember when I sat down at my desk in Adrian College (Adrian, Michigan) in the wake of the Newark and Detroit riots in July 1967. I could hardly contain my rage against the white church and its theology for their inability to see that the God of Jesus was at work in places they least expected—Black Power! That essay was the beginning of my theological journey. I was well aware of the risk I was taking in making such a radical break with my theological education. But with black people dying in the streets of America, I just could not keep silent. I had to speak a liberating word for my people. Once I took the first step, I kept on stepping—writing *Black Theology and Black Power* (1969) in a month's time in the summer of 1968.

In writing *Black Theology and Black Power*, I suddenly understood what Karl Barth must have felt when he first rejected the liberal theology of his professors in Germany. It was a liberating experience to be free of my liberal and neo-orthodox professors, to be liberated from defining theology with abstract theological jargon that was unrelated to the life-and-death issues of black people. Although separated by nearly fifty years and dealing with completely different theological situations and issues, I felt a spiritual kinship with Barth, especially in his writing of *The Epistle to the Romans* (1921) and in his public debate with Adolf Harnack, his former teacher.

As I think back to that time in the late 1960s, when white American theologians were writing and talking about the "death-of-God theology" as black people were fighting and dying in the streets, the energy swells once again. I was angry and could not keep it to myself. Like Malcolm X, I felt I was the angriest black theologian in America.[9] I had to speak out, as forcefully as I knew how, against the racism I witnessed in theology, the churches, and the broader society. And that was why I began to write.

Once I started writing I could not stop. The message I was seeking to communicate was "something like a burning fire shut up in my bones" (Jer. 20:9). I had to write or be consumed by my anger. As soon as I finished *Black Theology*, I dove immediately into writing *A Black Theology of Liberation* (1970). In the first book I addressed my race critique primarily to the white liberals in the church and society because they were the loudest in denouncing Black Power. White theology and the seminaries were a secondary concern. But as soon as I knew that I was leaving Adrian College to teach at Union Theological Seminary in New York, the most liberal and influential seminary in America, I decided that I had to address head-on white theology, the intellectual arm of the white church. Two of the world's most famous theologians had taught at Union—Reinhold Niebuhr and Paul Tillich. Although I respected their great intellectual contribution to theology and had learned much from their brilliant theological insights, I was not intimidated by their legacy. I was audacious enough to think that my understanding of the gospel was a simple truth, available to anyone who opened his/her heart and mind to the God revealed in the Scriptures and present in the world today. One does not need to be an intellectual giant to know that the God of the Bible is known as the liberator of the oppressed from physical and spiritual bondage. I did not regard this point as a brilliant insight. It was an obvious biblical truth and only white theologians' racism blinded them to it. In *A Black Theology of Liberation* I merely sought to remind them of it.

I did not limit my critique to white churches and their theologians. In *Black Theology and Black Power* I also leveled a sharp critique against the post–Civil War Black Church for its otherworldliness and indifference toward the political and cultural implication of Black Power. Black ministers were none too happy about that. To my surprise, even some black religion scholars questioned whether my focus on liberation was indigenous to the black religious experience or something I derived exclusively from the secular advocates of Black Power. "Black Spirituals: A Theological Interpretation" was my reply, followed by a book-length treatment on *The Spirituals and the Blues* (1972).

"Black Theology on Revolution, Violence, and Reconciliation" was written in the heat of theological debate and in the context of my involvement in the Black Power movement in the early 1970s. It was my standard address to white seminaries and churches that condemned Black Power as revolutionary and violent, saying it was unchristian. As the theologian of the Black Power movement, I felt that I had to give a theological reply to their misguided judgment.

"Black Theology and the Black Church: Where Do We Go from Here?" continues my affirmation and critique of the Black Church and also marks the beginning of a new development in my theological journey. Here I seek to connect the African-American struggle for justice with the struggles of the Third World poor in Africa, Asia, and Latin America. This is also the beginning of my recognition of the importance of Marxism as a tool of social analysis, largely through the influence of my dialogue with Latin American liberation theology in the Theology in the Americas (TIA) and the Ecumenical Association of Third World Theologians (EATWOT). Although our debates were heated (since I would not replace race with class as my starting point), I learned much from our dialogue.

The "Martin and Malcolm" section focuses on the two ministers most responsible for the rise of black liberation theology. Although I refer to them from the beginning of my reflections on black theology, they are not the subject of a sustained analysis. A disciplined investigation began in the 1980s with Martin King's theology where I was seeking to show that his thinking was primarily defined by the Black Church community and not white theology. I then proceeded to place him in conversation with Malcolm X, his most challenging critic. These essays were written before and after the publication of *Martin & Malcolm & America: A Dream or a Nightmare* (1991) and cover topics not developed there. All were presented as addresses at events celebrating Martin King's birthday and his significance for America and the church. Following the early focus on Martin's theology, I now almost never talk or write about Martin without giving similar attention to Malcolm. People are always asking me who of the two is the more important for my theological perspective. Some think Martin and others, Malcolm. I say both are equally important, because each contributes something essential to my theological identity.

The "Going Forward" section addresses the importance of solidarity across differences as we move into the next millennium. Nothing is more important than unity among black people and solidarity with all who are struggling to make a world that is safe and healthy for life in all its forms.

No issue is more urgent than the fight against patriarchy in the Black Church community. Unfortunately, I have not always been supportive of women in the ministry, at least not as forcefully as common sense and the gospel demanded. While I did not publicly oppose gender-consciousness in theology, I just kept silent about it and continued my writing and teaching about black liberation theology as if gender-inclusive language and black women's experience made no distinctive contribution to my understanding of liberation and its impact on theology. It was a sexist assumption, just as detrimental to humanity as racism. I was like white theologians who were silent about black theology. I broke my silence in the middle of the 1970s when black women students at Garrett-Evangelical Theological Seminary (October 1976) asked me to address a black women's conference on the theme "New Roles in the Ministry: A Theological Appraisal." It was my first halting effort. Since then, I have endeavored to always use inclusive language and engage gender issues in my teaching, writing, and way of life. Womanist theologians continue to challenge my thinking, reminding me that I still have a long way to go. I did not seek to remove the obviously male-centered language in my early essays, because I think it is important for me to acknowledge the limits of my perspective during the course of thirty years of writing.

In "Black Theology and the Black College Student" I address young blacks who were in danger of separating themselves from the religious roots of their elders. That danger is still present today. There is no future for the African-American community divided against itself. We need one another, the young and the elders, men and women, for together we stand and divided we fall.

I do not see any future for humankind unless people around the world come to their senses and learn how to treat one another as human beings. This is especially true for white people in relation to people of color. Unlike many black nationalists, past and present, I do not believe that whites by nature are more sinful than other people. They just have more power—intellectual, political, social, economic, military, and otherwise—to do evil. "Humans exhibit the greatest cruelty when they have uncurbed power to do so," especially "when mob or group actions override individual judgment and sensitivity."[10] As Reinhold Niebuhr was persistent in reminding us, powerful groups have very little capacity to restrain themselves from evil acts against the powerless.[11] No group has been more evil than whites, especially in relation to black people over such a long period of time. I emphasized this point nearly thirty years ago. What is still amazing to me is that white theologians and ethicists, the intellectual and spiritual conscience of America and the world, continue to write about everything under the sun *except* the cancer of racism. "White Theology Revisited" is another urgent call to white theologians to recognize that their theologies will never have integrity as long as they fail to incorporate a persistent and radical race critique in their discourse.

This same unity principle must be applied to the whole of humanity and indeed to life itself. Unless we learn how to live in harmony with one another and with the universe we will self-destruct. This is the central point of "Whose Earth Is It, Anyway?" presented at an ecology conference at Union Seminary.

Risks of Faith represents thirty years of searching for the truth of the gospel. I do not claim to have found the whole truth. I am still searching, for I know, as Paul knew, "we see in a mirror, dimly" and thus "know only in part," not fully (1 Cor. 13:12 New Revised Standard Version). The partial truths we see can be enlarged if we have the humility to open ourselves to the verity of other peoples' experiences. Let us hope that we will recognize our common humanity so that together we can create a world that is truly the "beloved community" of life.

Black Theology and Black Power

[Black Power] means that blacks accept the risk of defining themselves. Like our forefathers who rebelled against slavery, we know that life is not worth living unless we are fighting against its limits.

—The Christian Century, Sept. 16, 1970

I cannot de-emphasize the *literal* significance of blackness. My people were enslaved, lynched, and ghettoized in the name of God and country because of their color. No amount of theologizing can remove the reality of that experience from my consciousness. And because blacks were de-humanized by white-skinned people who created a cultural style based on black oppression, the *literal* importance of whiteness has historical referents.

—The Christian Century, Sept. 15, 1971

Christianity and Black Power

1967

M y purpose is to examine the concept of Black Power and its relationship to Christianity and the Church. Some religionists would consider Black Power the work of the Antichrist. Others would suggest that such a concept should be tolerated as an expression of Christian love to the misguided black brother. It is my thesis, however, that Black Power, even in its most radical expression, is not an antithesis of Christianity, nor is it a heretical idea to be tolerated with painful forbearance. It is rather Christ's central message to twentieth-century America. And unless the empirical denominational Church makes a determined effort to recapture the Man Jesus through a total identification with the suffering poor as expressed in Black Power, that Church will become exactly what Christ is not.

That most churches see an irreconcilable conflict between Christianity and Black Power is evidenced not only by the structure of their community (the 11:00 A.M. hour on Sunday is still the most segregated hour of any weekday), but by their typical response to riots: "I deplore the violence but sympathize with the reasons for the violence." What churchmen, laymen, and ministers alike apparently fail to recognize is their contribution to the ghetto-condition through permissive silence—except for a few resolutions which they usually pass once a year or immediately following a riot—and through their cotenancy with a dehumanizing social structure whose existence depends on the enslavement of black people. If the Church is to remain faithful to its Lord, it must make a decisive break with the structure of this society by launching a vehement attack on the evils of racism in all forms. It must become *prophetic*, demanding a radical change in the interlocking structures of this society.

Of course the Church must realize, in view of the Christian doctrine of man, that this is a dangerous task. But obedience to Christ is always costly. The time has come for the Church to challenge the power structure with

3

the power of the *gospel*, knowing that nothing less than *immediate* and *total* emancipation of all people is consistent with the message and style of Jesus Christ. The Church cannot afford to deplore the means that oppressed people use to break the chains of slavery because such language not only clouds the issue but also gives comfort and assistance to the oppressor. Therefore, the primary purpose of this essay is to show that embracing Black Power is not only possible but necessary, if the Church wants to remain faithful to the traditions of Christianity as disclosed in the person of Jesus Christ.

Definition of Black Power

What does Black Power mean? It means nothing other than full emancipation of black people from white oppression by whatever means black people deem necessary. The methods may include selective buying, boycotting, marching, or even rebellion. Black Power, therefore, means black freedom, black self-determination, wherein black people no longer view themselves as animals devoid of human dignity but as men, human beings with the ability to carve out their own destiny. In short, as Stokely Carmichael would say, Black Power means T.C.B., Take Care of Business—black folk taking care of black folks' business not on the terms of the oppressor, but on those of the oppressed.

Black Power is analogous to Albert Camus's understanding of the rebel. The rebel is the man who says no and yes; he says no to conditions considered intolerable, and yes to that "something within him which 'is worth while . . .' and which must be taken into consideration."[1] He says no to "the humiliating orders of his master," and by so doing testifies to that something that is placed above everything else, including life itself. To say no means that death is preferable to life, if the latter is devoid of freedom. In the words of the black spiritual, "Before I be a slave I'll be buried in my grave." This is what Black Power means.

Unfortunately, many well-intentioned persons have insisted that there must be another approach, one that will not cause so much hostility, not to mention rebellion. Therefore, appeal is made to the patience of black people to keep their "cool" and not to get carried away by their feelings. These men argue that if any progress is to be made, it will be through a careful, *rational* approach to the subject. These people are deeply offended when black people refuse to listen and place such liberals in the same category as the most adamant segregationists. They simply do not see that such reasoned appeals merely support the perpetuation of the ravaging of the black community. Black Power, in this respect, is by nature "*irrational*," that is, not denying the role of rational reflection, but insisting that human existence cannot be mechanized or put into neat boxes according to reason. Human reason, though valuable, is not absolute, because moral decisions—those decisions that deal with human dignity—cannot be made by using the *abstract* methods of science. Human emotions must be reckoned with. Consequently, black people must say no to all do-gooders who insist that they need more time. If such persons really knew oppression—knew it existentially in their guts—they would not be confused or disturbed at black rebellion, but would join black people in their fight for freedom and dignity. It is interesting that most people do understand why Jews can hate Germans. Why can they not also understand why black people, who have been deliberately and systematically murdered by the structure of this society, hate white people? The general failure of Americans to make this connection suggests that the primary difficulty is their inability to see black men as men. *No — I think it is because we can't conceive of ourselves as inhuman. It is to admit shame we would have to take responsibility*

This leads us to another reason why the concept of Black Power is rejected. Some persons would have us believe that advocating Black Power creates too much resentment or hate among black people and this makes significant personal relationship between black and white impossible. It should be obvious that the hate that black people feel toward white people is not due to the creation of the phrase *Black Power*. Rather it is a result of the deliberate and systematic ordering of society on the basis of racism, making black alienation not only possible but inevitable. For 350 years black people have been enslaved by the tentacles of white power, tentacles that worm their way into the guts of their being and "invade the gray cells of their cortex." For 350 years they have cried, waited, voted, marched, picketed, and boycotted, but whites still refuse to recognize their humanity. In light of this, attributing black resentment to the creation of Black Power is ridiculous, if not obscene. *like a run away father*

Furthermore, while it is true that black people do hate whites, it is misleading to suggest that hatred is essential to the definition of Black Power. Quoting Carmichael's denial of the "black supremacy" charge: "There is no analogy—by any stretch of definition or imagination—between the advocates of Black Power and white racists. . . . The goal of the racists is to keep black people on the bottom, arbitrarily and dictatorially, as they have done in this country for over three hundred years. The goal of black self-determination and black self-identity—Black Power—is full participation in the decision-making processes affecting the lives of black people."[2] In hate one desires something that is not his; but the black man's intention is to claim what is his—freedom. Therefore, it is not the purpose of the black man to repudiate his enslaver's dignity, but only his right as an enslaver. The rebellion in the cities should not be interpreted as the work of a few blacks who want something for nothing but as an assertion of the dignity of black people. The black man is assuming that there is a common value which is recognizable by all as existing in all people, and he is testifying to that *something* in his rebellion. He is expressing his solidarity with the human race.

In reality, then, *accommodation* and *protest* seem to be the only options open to the black man. For three hundred years he accommodated, thereby giving credence to his own enslavement. Black Power means that he will no longer accommodate; that he will no longer tolerate white excuses for enslavement; that he will no longer be guided by the oppressor's understanding of justice, liberty, freedom, or the methods to be used in attaining it. He recognizes the difference between theoretical equality and great factual inequalities. He will not sit by and wait for the white man's love to be extended to his black brother. He will protest, violently, if need be, on behalf of absolute and immediate emancipation. Black Power means that black people will cease trying rationally to articulate the political advantages and moral rightness of human freedom, because the dignity of man is a self-evident religious, philosophical, and political *truth*, without which human community is impossible. When one group breaks the accepted human covenant (i.e., a mutual respect for human freedom), it begins to plant the seeds of rebellion.

Many concerned persons have pointed out the futility of black rebellion by drawing a vast contrast between the present conditions of the black man in the ghetto and other revolutionaries of the past. They say that revolution depends on cohesion, discipline, stability, and the sense of a stake in society. The ghetto, by contrast, is relatively incohesive, unorganized, unstable and numerically too small to be effective. Therefore, rebellion for the black man can only mean extermination.

The analysis is essentially correct. But to point out the futility of rebellion is to miss the *point* of black rebellion. Black people know that they compose less than 12 percent of the total population and are proportionately weak with respect to economic, political, or military power. The rebellion in the cities is not a conscious organized attempt of black people to take over; it is an attempt to say *yes* to their own dignity even in death. Therefore, the question is not whether black people are prepared to die—the riots testify to that—but whether whites are prepared to kill them. Unfortunately, it seems that that answer has been given through the riots as well. Yet this willingness of black people to die is not novel but is rather a part of the heritage of Christianity.

Christianity and Black Power

The black intellectual community is becoming increasingly suspicious of Christianity because the oppressor has used it as a means of directing the oppressed away from any concern for present inequalities by emphasizing a heavenly reality beyond time and space. Naturally, as the slave begins to question his existence as a slave, he also questions the religion of the enslaver.

It is, therefore, appropriate to ask, "Is Black Power compatible with the Christian faith, or are we dealing with two radically divergent perspectives?" To answer these questions we need to ask and answer a prior question: "What is Christianity?"

Christianity begins and ends with the Man Jesus—his life, death, and resurrection. He is the essence of Christianity. Schleiermacher was not far wrong when he said that "Christianity is essentially distinguished from other faiths by the fact that everything in it is related to the redemption accomplished by Jesus of Nazareth."[3] In contrast to many religions, Christianity revolves around a Person, without whom its existence ceases to be. Christ and Christianity belong together; they cannot be separated. Granted, there have been historical disagreements regarding the nature of that connection. The relationship has been conceived as inward or as external and mechanical. But it is impossible to separate Christ from Christianity without robbing it of its uniqueness.

The central importance of Jesus Christ for Christianity is plainest of all when we consider the New Testament picture of Jesus. According to the New Testament, Jesus is the man for others who views his existence as inextricably tied to other men to the degree that his own Person is inexplicable apart from others. *Others*, of course, refers to all men, especially the oppressed, the unwanted of society, the sinners. He is God Himself coming into the very depths of human existence for the sole purpose of destroying all human tentacles of slavery, thereby freeing man from ungodly principalities and powers that hinder his relationship with God. Jesus himself defines the nature of his ministry in these terms:

> The Spirit of the Lord is upon me,
> because he has anointed me to preach the good news to the poor,
> He has sent me to proclaim release to the captives and recovering of
>   sight to the blind,
> To set at liberty those who are oppressed,
> To proclaim the acceptable year of the Lord.
>
> *(Luke 4:18, 19)*

His work is essentially one of liberation. Becoming a slave himself, he opens realities of human existence formerly closed to man. Through an encounter with him, man now knows the full meaning of God's action in history and man's place within it.

The Gospel of Mark describes the nature of Jesus' ministry in this manner: "The time is fulfilled, the Kingdom of God is at hand; repent and believe the Gospel" (1:14, 15). On the face of it this message appears not to be too radical to our twentieth-century ears, but this impression stems from our failure existentially to bridge the gap between modern man and biblical man. In reality the message of the Kingdom strikes at the very center of man's desire to define his own existence in the light of his own interest at the price of his brother's enslavement. It means the irruption of a new age, an age that has to do with God's action in history on behalf of man's salvation. It is an age of liberation, in which "the blind receive their sight, the lame walk, the lepers are cleansed, the deaf hear, the dead are raised up, the poor have the good news preached to them" (Luke 7:22). This is not pious talk, and one does not need a seminary degree to interpret the passage. It is a message about the ghetto, Vietnam, and all other injustices done in the name of democracy and religion to further the social, political, and economic interests of the oppressor. In Christ, God enters human affairs and takes sides with the oppressed. Their suffering becomes his; their despair, divine despair. Through Christ the poor are offered freedom now to rebel against that which makes them other than human.

It is ironical that America with its history of injustice to the poor (especially regarding the black man and the Indian) prides itself as a Christian nation (is there really such an animal?). It is even more ironical that officials within the body of the Church have passively or actively participated in injustices. With Jesus, however, the poor were at the heart of his mission: "The last shall be first and the first last" (Matt. 20:16). That is why he was always kind to traitors, adulterers, and sinners and why the Samaritan came out on top in the parable. Speaking of Pharisees (the religiously elite of his day), he said: "Truly I say to you, the tax collectors (traitors) and harlots go into the Kingdom—but not you" (Matt. 21:31). Jesus had little tolerance for the middle- or upper-class religious snob whose attitude attempted to usurp the sovereignty of God and destroy the dignity of the poor. The Kingdom is for the poor and not the rich because the former has nothing to expect from the world while the latter's entire existence is grounded in his commitment to worldly things. The poor man may expect everything from God while the rich man may expect nothing because of his refusal to free himself from his own pride. It is not that poverty is a precondition for entrance into the Kingdom. But those who recognize their utter dependence on God and wait on him despite the miserable absurdity of life are usually poor, according to our Lord. And the Kingdom which the poor may enter is not merely an eschatological longing for escape to a transcendent reality, nor is it an inward serenity that eases unbearable suffering. Rather it is God encountering man in the very depths of his being-in-the-world and releasing him from all human evils, like racism, which hold him captive. The repentant man knows that even though God's ultimate Kingdom is in the future, it breaks through even now like a ray of light upon the darkness of the oppressed.

When we make it contemporaneous with our life situation, Jesus' message is clear enough. The message of Black Power is the message of Christ himself. To be sure, that statement is both politically and religiously dangerous. It is so politically because Black Power threatens the very structure of the American way of life. It is theologically dangerous because it may appear to overlook Barth's early emphasis on "the infinite qualitative distinction between God and man." In this regard, we must say that Christ never promised political security, but the opposite; and Karl Barth was mainly concerned with the easy identification of the work of God with the work of the State. But if Luther's statement "we are Christ to the neighbor" is to be taken seriously, and if we can believe the New Testament witness that proclaims Jesus as resurrected and thus active even now in the midst of human misery, then he must be alive in men who are where the action is. If the gospel is a gospel of liberation for the oppressed, then Jesus is where the oppressed are. Jesus is not safely confined in the first century. He is our contemporary, proclaiming release to the captives and rebelling against all who silently accept the structure. If perchance he is not in the ghetto, if he is not where men are living at the brink of existence, but is rather in the easy life of the suburb, then he lied and Christianity is a mistake. Christianity, therefore, is not alien to Black Power; it *is* Black Power!

There are perhaps many secular interpretations that could account for the present black rebellion as there were secular views of the Exodus or of the life and death of Jesus. But for the Christian, there is only one interpretation: Black rebellion is God himself actively involved in the present-day affairs of men for the purpose of liberating a people. Through his work, black people now know that there is something more important than life itself. They can afford to be indifferent toward death, because life devoid of freedom is not worth living.

The Church and Black Power

What is the Church and its relationship to Christ and Black Power? According to the New Testament, the Church is the *laos theou*, the "people of God." It is a community of people who have encountered God's action in history and thus desire to participate in Christ's continued work of liberation. As Bonhoeffer puts it, the Church is "Christ existing as community" or Christ's "presence in history." This means that the Church's work and message is nothing other than a continuation of the message and work of Christ. It is, as Barth puts it, "God's provisional demonstration of his intention for all humanity."

If the real Church is the *laos theou* whose primary task is that of being Christ to the world by proclaiming the message of the gospel *(kerygma)*, by rendering services of liberation *(diakonia)*, and by being itself a manifestation of the nature of the new society *(koinonia)*, then the empirical Church has failed on all counts. It certainly has not rendered service of reconciliation to the poor, evidently because it represents the values of a sick society that oppresses the poor. Some present-day theologians, like Hamilton and Altizer, taking their cue from Nietzsche and the present irrelevancy of the Church to modern man, have announced the death of God. It seems, however, that their chief mistake lies in their apparent identification of God's reality with the signed-up Christians. If we were to identify the work of God with the denominational Church, then, like Altizer, we must "will the death of God with a passion of faith." Or as Camus would say, taking his cue from Bakunin, "If God *did* exist, we should have to abolish Him!"

The Church has not only failed to render service to the poor, but also failed miserably at being a visible manifestation of God's intention for humanity and at proclaiming the message of the gospel to the world. It seems that the Church is not God's redemptive agent but rather an agent of the old society. It not only fails to create an atmosphere for radical obedience to Christ, but also precludes the possibility of becoming a loyal, devoted servant of God. How else can we explain that some church fellowships are more concerned with nonsmoking principles or temperances than with children who die of rat bites or men who are shot while looting a TV set. Men are dying of hunger, children are maimed from rat bites, women are dying of despair, and churches pass resolutions. While we may have difficulty in locating the source of evil, we know what must be done against evil in order to relieve the suffering of the poor. We know why men riot. Perhaps we cannot prevent riots, but we can fight against conditions that cause them. The Church is placed in question because of its contribution to a structure that produces riots.

Some churchmen may reply: "We do condemn the deplorable conditions which produce urban riots. We do condemn racism and all the evils arising from it." But to the extent that this is true, the Church, with the exception of a few isolated individuals, voices its condemnation in the style of resolutions that are usually equivocal and almost totally unproductive. If the condemnation was voiced, it was not understood! The Church should speak in a style that avoids abstractions. Its language should be backed up with relevant involvement in the affairs of people who suffer. It must be a grouping whose community life and personal involvement are coherent with its language about the gospel.

The Church does not appear to be a community willing to pay up personally. It is not a community that views every command of Jesus as a call to the cross—death. Rather, it is an institution whose existence depends on the evils that produce the riots in the cities. With this in mind, we must say that when a minister blesses by silence the conditions that produce riots and condemns the rioters, he gives up his credentials as a Christian minister and becomes inhuman. He is an animal, just like those who, backed by an ideology of racism, order the structure of this society on the basis of white supremacy. We need men who refuse to be animals and are resolved to pay the price, so that all men can be something more than animals.

Whether Black Power advocates are that grouping, we will have to wait and see. But the Church has shown many times that it loves life and is not prepared to die for others. It has not really gone where the action is with a willingness to die for the neighbor, but remains aloof from the sufferings of men. It is a ministry to middle-class America! How else can one explain its snail-like pace toward an inclusive membership? Even though Paul says that Christ "has broken down the dividing walls of hostility" (Eph. 2:14), the Church's community life reflects racism through and through. It is still possible to be a racist, a black-hater, and at the same time a member of the Church. It is my contention that the Church cannot be the Church of Christ and sponsor or even tolerate racism. The fact that the Church does indeed tolerate or sponsor racism is evidenced by its *whiteness*.

This leads me to conclude that Christ is operating outside the denominational Church. The real Church of Christ is that grouping that identifies with the suffering of the poor by becoming one with them. While we should be careful in drawing the line, the line must nevertheless be drawn. The Church includes not only the Black Power community but all men who view their humanity as inextricably related to every man. It is that grouping with a demonstrated willingness to die for the prevention of the torture of others, saying with Bonhoeffer, "when Christ calls a man, he bids him come and die."

Which church? black, white, both,

Black Spirituals:
A Theological Interpretation

Contrary to popular opinion, the spirituals are not evidence that black people reconciled themselves with human slavery. On the contrary, they are black freedom songs that emphasize black liberation as consistent with divine revelation. For this reason, it is most appropriate for black people to sing them in this "new" age of Black Power. And if some people still regard the spirituals as inconsistent with Black Power and black theology, that is because they have been misguided and the songs misinterpreted. There is little evidence that black slaves accepted their servitude because they believed God willed their slavery. The opposite is the case. The spirituals speak of God's liberation of black people, his will to set right the oppression of black slaves despite the overwhelming power of white masters. . . .

And if "de God dat lived in Moses' time is jus de same today," then that God will vindicate the suffering of the righteous black and punish the unrighteous whites for their wrongdoings.

A large amount of scholarship has been devoted to the music and poetry of the black spiritual, but little has been written about its theology. Apparently most scholars assume that the value of the black spiritual lies in its artistic expression and not its theological content, which could be taken to mean that blacks can "sing and dance good" but cannot think. For example, almost everyone agrees with W. E. B. Du Bois's contention that "the Negro is primarily an artist"[1] and that his gift of music to America is unsurpassed. But what about the black person as a philosopher and theologian? Is it not possible that the thought of the spiritual is as profound as its music is creative, since without thought art is impossible? In this essay my purpose is to investigate the theological implications of the black spirituals, with special reference to the meaning of God, Jesus Christ, suffering, and eschatology.

I

No theological interpretation of the black spirituals is valid that ignores the cultural environment that created them, and understanding a culture means, in part, perceiving its history. Black history in America is a history of black servitude, a record of pain and sorrows, slave ships and auction blocks. It is the story of black life in chains and of what that meant for the souls and bodies of black people. This is the history that created the spirituals, and it must be recognized if we are to render a valid theological interpretation of these black songs.

The logical place to begin is 1619 when twenty black Africans were sold as indentured servants at Jamestown, Virginia. Actually, there was nothing historically unusual about that event, since indentured servitude was already in existence, and many whites were victims. But in 1661 the significance of 1619 was clearly defined when Virginia legalized black slavery, declaring that people of African descent would be slaves for life. Maryland legalized black slavery two years later, and soon after all colonies followed suit. America became the land of the free for white people only, and for blacks she became a land of bondage.

Physical slavery was cruel. It meant working fifteen to twenty hours per day and being beaten unmercifully if one displayed the slightest fatigue. The auction block became a symbol of "brokenness" because no family ties were recognized. Husbands were separated from wives and children from parents. There were few laws protecting the slaves, since most whites believed that Africans were only partly human (three-fifths was the fraction fixed by the Fathers in 1787). Later, to put down any lingering doubts, the highest court of the land decreed that black people had no rights that white people were bound to respect. Slaves were property, as were animals and objects; their owners could dispose of them as they saw fit—provided they did not endanger the welfare of the society as a whole.

It has been said that not all masters were cruel, and perhaps there is some truth in the observation—particularly if it is made from a perspective that does not know the reality of the slave-experience. But from the black perspective, the phrase "good" master is an absurdity, a logical contradiction. To speak of "good" masters is like speaking of "good" racists and "good" murderers. Who in their right minds could make such nonsensical distinctions, except those who deal in historical abstractions? Certainly not the victims! Indeed, it may be argued that the so-called good masters were in fact the worst, if we consider the dehumanizing effect of mental servitude. At least those who were blatant in their physical abuse did not camouflage their savagery with Christian doctrine, and it may have been easier for black slaves to make the necessary value-distinctions so that they could regulate their lives according to black definitions. But "good" Christian masters could cover up their brutality by rationalizing it with Christian theology, making it difficult for slaves to recognize the demonic. Undoubtedly, white Christianity contributed to the phenomenon of "house niggers" (not all domestic servants were in this category), those blacks who internalized the masters' values, revealing information about insurrections planned by their brothers. The "good" masters convinced them that slavery was their lot ordained by God, and it was his will for blacks to be obedient to white people. After all, Ham was cursed, and St. Paul did admonish slaves to be obedient to their masters.

Initially, white masters did not permit their slaves to be Christianized. Christian baptism implied manumission, according to some; and there were too many biblical references to freedom. But white missionaries and preachers convinced slavemasters that Christianity made blacks "better" slaves—obedient and docile. As one slaveholder put it: "The deeper the piety of the slave, the more valuable he is in every respect."[2] White Christianity assisted in the internalization of white values in the minds of slaves, reconciling them to the condition of servitude. The Christianity taught to black slaves was a distorted interpretation of the gospel, geared to the ideological enforcement of white racism. Black resistance to slavery was interpreted as sin; revolt against the master was said to be revolt against God, and that could only mean eternal damnation. To be sure, Christianity offered freedom, but for slaves it was interpreted to mean freedom from sin, the lust and passion that made them disregard the interests of their masters. Such was the history that created the spirituals.

II

But the history that created the spirituals contains much more than what white people *did* to black people. Black history is also the record of black people's historical strivings, an account of their perceptions of their existence in an oppressive society. What whites did to blacks is secondary. The primary reality is what blacks did to whites in order to restrict the white assault on their humanity.

When white people enslaved Africans, their intention was to dehistoricize black existence, to foreclose the possibility of a future defined by the African heritage. White people demeaned the sacred tales of the black fathers, ridiculing their myths and defiling the sacred rites. Their intention was to define man according to European definitions so that their brutality against Africans could be characterized as civilizing the savages. But white Europeans did not succeed, and black history is the record of their failure. Black people did not stand by passively while white oppressors demoralized their being. Many rebelled—physically and mentally. Black history in America is the history of that rebellion.

Black rebellion in America did not begin with the Civil Rights movement and Martin Luther King, nor with Black Power and Stokely Carmichael or the Black Panther Party. Black resistance has roots stretching back to the auction blocks and the slave codes. It began when the first black person decided that death would be preferable to slavery. If white government officials could just realize this, then they might be able to understand the Black Panthers and other black revolutionaries. White people should know about Harriet Tubman and her liberation of more than three hundred black slaves. They should know about Henry Garnett and his urgent call for rebellion among the slaves. Black slaves were not passive, and black history is the record of their physical resistance against the condition of human bondage.

To understand the history of black resistance, it is also necessary to know the black spirituals. They are historical songs that speak about the rupture of black lives; they tell us about a people in the land of bondage and what they did to hold themselves together and to fight back. We are told that the people of Israel could not sing the Lord's song in a strange land. But, for blacks, their *Being* depended upon a song. Through song, they built new structures for existence in an alien land. The spirituals enabled blacks to retain a measure of African identity while living in the midst of American slavery, providing both the substance and the rhythm to cope with human servitude.

Much has been said about the compensatory and otherworldly ideas in the black spirituals. While I do not question the presence of that theme, there is, nevertheless, another train of thought running through these songs. And unless this emphasis is considered, it is possible that the spirituals cannot be understood. I am referring to the emphasis on freedom in this world, and the kinds of risks blacks were willing to take in order to attain it.

> *Oh Freedom! Oh Freedom!*
> *Oh Freedom, I love thee!*
> *And before I'll be a slave,*
> *I'll be buried in my grave,*
> *And go home to my Lord and be free.*

The theme of freedom and activities it implied explains why slaveholders did not allow black slaves to worship and sing their songs unless authorized white people were present to proctor the meeting. And after the Nat Turner revolt, black preachers were declared illegal in most southern states. Black religious gatherings were often occasions for organizing resistance against the institution of slavery.

Black history is the stuff out of which the black spirituals were created. But the "stuff" of black history includes more than the bare historical facts of slavery. Black history is an experience, a soulful event. And to understand it is to know the Being of a people who had to "feel their way along the course of American slavery,"[3] enduring the stresses and strains of human servitude but not without a song. *Black history is a spiritual!*

III

The divine liberation of the oppressed from slavery is the central theological concept in the black spirituals. These songs show that black slaves did not believe that human servitude was reconcilable with their African past and their knowledge of the Christian gospel. They did not believe that God created Africans to be the slaves of Europeans. Accordingly they sang of a God who was involved in history—*their* history—making right what whites have made wrong. Just as God delivered Moses and the Children of Israel from Egyptian bondage, drowning Pharaoh and his army in the Red

Sea, so also he will deliver black people from American slavery. It is this certainty that informs the thought of the black spirituals, enabling black slaves to sing:

> Oh Mary, don't you weep, don't you moan,
> Oh Mary, don't you weep, don't you moan,
> Pharaoh's army got drownded,
> Oh Mary, don't you weep.

The basic idea of the spirituals is that slavery contradicts God; it is a denial of His will. To be enslaved is to be declared *nobody,* and that form of existence contradicts God's creation of men to be his children. Because black people believed that they were God's children, they affirmed their *somebodiness,* refusing to reconcile their servitude with divine revelation. They rejected white distortions of the gospel, which emphasized the obedience of slaves to their masters. They contended that God willed their freedom and not their slavery. That is why the spirituals focus on biblical passages that stress God's involvement in the liberation of oppressed people. Black people sang about Joshua and the battle of Jericho, Moses leading the Israelites from bondage, Daniel in the lions' den, and the Hebrew children in the fiery furnace. Here the emphasis is on God's liberation of the weak from the oppression of the strong, the lowly and downtrodden from the proud and mighty. And blacks reasoned that if God could lock the lion's jaw for Daniel and could cool the fire for the Hebrew children, then he certainly could deliver black people from slavery.

> My Lord delivered Daniel
> Why can't He deliver me?

Contrary to popular opinion, the spirituals are not evidence that black people reconciled themselves with human slavery. On the contrary, they are black freedom songs which emphasize black liberation as consistent with divine revelation. For this reason it is most appropriate for black people to sing them in this "new" age of Black Power. And if some people still regard the spirituals as inconsistent with Black Power and black theology, that is because they have been misguided and the songs misinterpreted. There is little evidence that black slaves accepted their servitude because they believed God willed their slavery. The opposite is the case. The spirituals speak of God's liberation of black people, His will to set right the oppression of black slaves despite the overwhelming power of white masters. For blacks believed that there is an omnipotent, omnipresent, and omniscient power at work in the world, and that he is on the side of the oppressed and downtrodden. As evidence they pointed to the blind man who received his sight, the lame who walked, and Lazarus who was received into God's Kingdom while the rich man was rejected. And if "de God dat lived in Moses' time is jes' de same today," then that God will vindicate the suffering of the righteous blacks and punish the unrighteous whites for their wrongdoings.

IV

Some will argue, with Marx, that the very insistence upon *divine* activity is always evidence that people are helpless and passive. "Religion is the sign of the oppressed creature, the heart of the heartless world . . . the spirit of a spiritless situation. It is the *opium* of the people."[4] There were doubtless some black slaves who *literally* waited on God, expecting him to effect their liberation in response to their faithful passivity; but there is another side of the black experience to be weighed. When it is considered that Nat Turner, Denmark Vesey, and Harriet Tubman may have been creators of some of the spirituals, that "Sinner, please don't let this harvest pass" probably referred to a slave resistance meeting,[5] that after 1831 over two thousand slaves escaped yearly,[6] and that black churches interpreted civil disobedience as consistent with religion, then it is most likely that many slaves recognized the need for their own participation in God's liberation. Indeed, many believed that the only hands that God had were their hands, and without the risk of escape or insurrection, slavery would never end. This may be the meaning of the song, "Singin' wid a sword in ma han'." The sword may be the symbol of the need of black slaves to strike a blow for freedom even though the odds were against them. Certainly the strict enforcement of the slave codes and the merciless beating of many slaves who sang spirituals tend to point in that direction.[7] What is certain is that Christianity did not dull the drive for liberation among all black slaves, and there is much evidence that slaves appropriated the gospel to their various styles of resistance.

Seeking to detract from the theological significance of the spirituals, some critics may point out that black slaves were literalists in their interpretation of the Scripture, and this probably accounts for their acceptance of the white masters' interpretation of the Bible. Of course, it is true that

slaves were not biblical critics and were unaware of erudite white reflections on the origins of biblical writings. Like most of their contemporaries,
they accepted the inerrancy of Scripture. But the critical point is that their
very literalism supported a black gospel of earthly freedom. They were literal when they sang about Daniel in the lions' den, David and Goliath, and
Samson and the Philistines. On the other hand, they dispensed with biblical literalism when white people began to use the curse of Ham and Paul
as evidence that blacks ought to accept their slavery. As one ex-slave
preacher put it:

> When I starts preaching I couldn't read or write and had to preach
> what Master told me, and he say tell them niggers iffen they obeys the
> master they goes to Heaven; but I knowed there's something better for
> them, but daren't tell them 'cept on the sly. That I done lots. I tells 'em
> iffen they keeps praying, the Lord will set 'em free.[8]

Black slaves were not naive as is often supposed. They knew that slavery
contradicted humanity and divinity, and that was why they cited biblical
references that focused on the liberation of the oppressed. They believed
that God would deliver them. As he once locked the lion's jaw for Daniel,
he would paralyze the power of white masters.

> *Who lock, who lock de lion,*
> *Who lock, de lion's jaw?*
> *God, lock, God lock de lion's jaw.*

The point is clear. God is the liberator, the deliverer of the weak from the
injustice of the strong.

It is significant that theology proper blends imperceptibly into christology in the spirituals. No theological distinction is made between the Son
and the Father. Jesus is understood as the King, the deliverer of men from
unjust suffering. He is the comforter in time of trouble, the lily of the valley,
and the bright morning star.

> *He's King of Kings, and Lord of Lords,*
> *Jesus Christ, the first and last*
> *No man works like him.*

The death and resurrection of Jesus are particular focal points of the
spirituals. The death of Jesus meant that the savior died on the cross for
black slaves. His death was a symbol of their suffering, their trials and trib-

ulation in an unfriendly world. When Jesus was nailed to the cross and the Romans pierced him in the side, he was not alone; blacks suffered and died with him. That was why they sang:

> *Were you there when they crucified my Lord?*
> *Were you there when they crucified my Lord?*
> *Oh! sometimes it causes me to tremble, tremble, tremble;*
> *Were you there when they crucified my Lord?*

Black slaves were there! Through the experience of being slaves, they encountered the theological significance of Jesus' death. With the crucifixion, Jesus makes an unqualified identification with the poor and helpless and takes their pain upon himself. They were there at the crucifixion because his death was for them.

And if Jesus was not alone in his suffering, they also were not alone in their slavery. Jesus is with them! Herein lies the meaning of the resurrection. It means that Jesus is not dead but is alive.

> *He rose, he rose from the dead,*
> *An' de Lord shall bear my spirit hom'.*

The resurrection is the divine guarantee that their lives are in the hands of him who conquered death, enabling men to do what is necessary to remain obedient to the Father, the creator and sustainer of life.

V

Though black slaves believed that the God of Jesus Christ was involved in the historical liberation of oppressed people from bondage, the continued existence of American slavery seemed to contradict that belief. If God was omnipotent and in control of human history, how could His goodness be reconciled with human servitude? If God had the power to deliver black people from the evil of slavery as he delivered Moses from Pharaoh's army, Daniel from the lions' den, and the Hebrew children from the fiery furnace, why then were black slaves still subject to the rule of white masters? Why are we still living in wretched conditions when God could end this evil thing with one righteous stroke?

These are hard questions, and they are still relevant today. In the history of theology and philosophy, these questions are the core of the "problem of evil"; college and seminary professors have spent many hours debating them. But black slaves did not have the opportunity to investigate the problem of suffering in the luxury of a seminar room with all the comforts of modern living. They encountered suffering in the cotton fields of Georgia, Arkansas, and Mississippi. Under the whip and pistol, they had to deal with the absurdities of human existence. Every time they opened their eyes and visualized the contradictions of their environment, they realized they were "rolling through an unfriendly world." How could a good and powerful God be reconciled with white masters and overseers? What explanation could the Holy One of Israel give for allowing the existence of an ungodly slave institution?

In order to understand the black slave's reaction to his enslavement, it is necessary to point out that his reflections on the problem of suffering were not "rational" in the classical Greek sense, with an emphasis on abstract and universal distinctions between good and evil, justice and injustice. The black slave had little time for reading books or sitting in the cool of the day, thinking about neat philosophical answers to the problem of evil. It was not only illegal to teach slaves to read, but most were forced to work from daybreak to nightfall, leaving no spare time for the art of theological and philosophical discourse. The black slave's investigation of the absurdities of human existence was concrete, and it was done within the context of the community of faith. No attempt was made to transcend the faith of the community by assuming a universal stance common to "all" men. In this sense, his reflection on human suffering was not unlike the biblical view of Yahweh's activity in human history. It was grounded in the historical realities of communal experience.

The classic examples in biblical history are found in the prophet Habakkuk and the sage Job. Both raised questions about the justice of God, but they were clearly questions for the faithful—not for philosophers. They took on significance only if one were a member of the community of faith. Habakkuk was concerned about the violence and the destruction of the land as witnessed in the army of the Chaldeans, while Job questioned the deuteronomic success formula. But in each case, the ultimate sovereignty of God was not denied. What was requested was a divine explanation so that the faithful could understand the ways of the Almighty. There was no philosophical resolution of the problem of evil. Suffering was a reality of life, and the believer must be able to take it upon himself without losing faith.

VI

In the spirituals, the slave's experience of suffering and despair defines for him the major issue in his view of the world. He does not really question the justice and goodness of God. He takes for granted God's righteousness and vindication of the poor and weak. Indeed, it is the point of departure for his faith. The slave has another concern, centered on the *faithfulness* of the community of believers in a world full of trouble. He wonders not whether God is just and right but whether the sadness and pain of the world will cause him to lose heart and thus fall prey to the ways of evil. He is concerned about the *togetherness* of the community of sufferers. Will the wretched of the earth be able to experience the harsh realities of despair and loneliness and take this pain upon themselves and not lose faith in the gospel of God? There was no attempt to evade the reality of suffering. Black slaves faced the reality of the world "ladened wid trouble, an' burden'd wid grief," but they believed that they could go to Jesus in secret and get relief. They appealed to Jesus not so much to remove the trouble (though that was included), but to keep them from "sinkin' down."

Significantly, the note of despair is usually intertwined with confidence and joy that "trouble don't last always." To be sure, the slave sings, "Sometimes I feel like a motherless child, a long way from home"; but because he is confident that Jesus is with him and has not left him completely alone, he can still add (in the same song!), "Glory Hallelujah!" The black slaves did not deny the experience of agony and loneliness in a world filled with trouble.

> *Nobody knows the trouble I've seen,*
> *Nobody knows my sorrow.*
> *Nobody knows the trouble I've seen,*
> *Glory, Hallelujah!*

The "Glory, Hallelujah!" is not a denial of trouble; it is an affirmation of faith. It says that despite the pain of being alone in an unfriendly world the black slave is confident that God has not really left him, and *trouble* is not the last word on human existence.

> *Soon-a-will be done with the trouble of the world;*
> *Soon-a-will be done with the trouble of the world;*
> *Going home to live with God.*

It appears that the slave is not concerned with the problem of evil per se, as if he intuitively knows that nothing will be solved through a debate of that problem. He deals with the world as it *is*, not as it might have been if God had acted "justly." He focuses on present realities of despair and loneliness that disrupt the community of faith. The faithful seems to have lost faith, and he experiences the agony of being alone in a world of hardship and pain. That is why he sings:

> *I couldn't hear nobody pray.*
> *Oh I couldn't hear nobody pray.*
> *Oh way down yonder by myself,*
> *And I couldn't hear nobody pray.*

VII

Related to the problem of suffering was the future, the "not-yet" of black existence. How was it possible for black slaves to take seriously their pain and suffering in an unfriendly world and still believe that God was liberating them from earthly bondage? How could they *really* believe that God was just when they knew only injustice and oppression? The answer to these questions lies in the concept of heaven, which is the dominant idea in black religious experience as expressed in the black spirituals.

The concept of heaven in black religion has not been interpreted rightly. Most observers have defined the black religious experience exclusively in terms of slaves longing for heaven, as if that desire were unrelated to their earthly liberation. It has been said that the concept of heaven served as an opiate for black slaves, making for docility and submission. But to interpret black eschatology solely in terms of its outmoded cosmology fails to take seriously the culture and thought of a people seeking expression amidst the dehumanization of slavery. It is like discarding the Bible and its message as irrelevant because the biblical writers had a three-storied conception of the universe. While not all biblical and systematic theologians agree with Rudolf Bultmann's method of demythologization in his efforts to solve the problem of biblical mythology, most agree that he is correct in his insistence that the gospel message is not dependent on its pre-scientific world-picture. Is it not possible that the same analogy is true in regard to the heaven theme in the spirituals?

Let me admit, then, that the black slaves' picture of the world is not to be defended as a viable scientific analysis of reality; that their image of the Promised Land, where "the streets are pearl and the gates are gold," is not the best way of communicating to contemporary Black Power advocates with their stress on political liberation by any means necessary; that a "new" black theological language is needed if black religion is going to be involved in articulating the historical strivings of black people in America and the Third World; and that the language of heaven is a white concept given to black slaves in order to make them obedient and submissive. The question nevertheless remains: How was it possible for black people to endure the mental and physical stresses of slavery and still keep their humanity intact? I think the answer is found in black eschatology; and maybe what is needed is not a dismissal of the idea of heaven but a reinterpretation of this concept so that oppressed blacks today can develop styles of resistance not unlike those of their grandparents.

VIII

The place to begin is Miles Fisher's contention that the spirituals are primarily "historical documents." They tell us about the black movement for historical liberation, the attempt of black people to define their present history in the light of their promised future, not according to their past miseries. Fisher notes that heaven for early black slaves referred not only to a transcendent reality beyond time and space; it designated the earthly places that blacks regarded as lands of freedom. Heaven referred to Africa, Canada, and the states north of the Mason-Dixon line.[9] Frederick Douglass wrote about the double meaning of these songs:

> We were at times remarkably buoyant, singing hymns, and making joyous exclamations, almost as triumphant in their tone as if we had reached a land of freedom and safety. A keen observer might have detected in our repeated singing of
>
> > O Canaan, sweet Canaan,
> > I am bound for the land of Canaan,
>
> something more than a hope of reaching heaven. We meant to reach the *North*, and the North was our Canaan.[10]

But while it is true that heaven had its historical referents, not all black slaves could hope to make it to Africa, Canada, or even to the northern section of the United States. The failure of the American Colonization Society's experiments crushed the hopes of many black slaves who were expecting to return to their African homeland. And blacks also began to realize that the North was not as significantly different from the South as they had envisioned, particularly in view of the Fugitive Slave Act of 1850 and the Dred Scott Decision in 1857. Black slaves began to realize that their historical freedom could not be assured as long as white racists controlled the governmental process of America. And so they found it necessary to develop a style of freedom that included but did not depend upon historical possibilities. What could freedom mean for black slaves who could never expect to participate in the determination of society's laws governing their lives? Must they continue to define freedom in terms of the possibility of escape and insurrection as if their humanity depended on their willingness to commit suicide? It was in response to this situation that the black concept of heaven developed.

For black slaves, who were condemned to carve out their existence in human captivity, heaven meant that the eternal God has made a decision about their humanity that could not be destroyed by white slavemasters. Whites could drive them, beat them, and even kill them; but they believed that God nevertheless had chosen black slaves as his own and that this election bestowed upon them a freedom to *be*, which could not be measured by what oppressors could do to the physical body. Whites may suppress black history and define Africans as savages, but the words of slavemasters do not have to be taken seriously when the oppressed know that they have a *somebodiness* that is guaranteed by the heavenly Father who alone is the ultimate sovereign of the universe. This is what heaven meant for black slaves.

The idea of heaven provided ways for black people to affirm their humanity when other people were attempting to define them as nonpersons. It enabled blacks to say yes to their right to be free by affirming God's eschatological freedom to be for the oppressed. That was what they meant when they sang about a "city called heaven."

> I am a poor pilgrim of sorrow.
> I'm in this world alone.
> No hope in this world for tomorrow.
> I'm trying to make heaven my home.

Sometimes I am tossed and driven.
Sometimes I don't know where to roam.
I've heard of a city called heaven.
I've started to make it my home.

In the midst of economic and political disfranchisement, black slaves held themselves together and did not lose their spiritual composure because they believed that their worth transcended governmental decisions. That was why they looked forward to "walking in Jerusalem just like John" and longed for the "camp meeting in the Promised Land."

IX

Despite the ways that black eschatology might have been misused or the crude forms in which it was sometimes expressed, it nevertheless provides us today with the best theological foundation for enabling American theologians to develop a concept of the future that is related to black oppression. Black theologians have little patience with so-called political theologians of America who say that they are concerned about humanizing the world according to God's promised future but do not relate that future to the history and culture of that people who have been and are being dehumanized and dehistoricized by white overlords. With all the talk among American theologians about "hope theology," "humanistic messianism," "Marxist-Christian dialogue," and revolutionary theology, one would expect that such language could easily be related to black people and their thoughts on eschatology and divine liberation. But white American theologians have been virtually silent on black liberation, preferring instead to do theology in the light of a modern liberalism that assumes that black people want to integrate into the white way of life. Such silence is inexcusable, and it is hard not to conclude that they are enslaved by their own identity with the culture and history of white slavemasters. What they need is liberation, and this can only happen when they face the reality of Black Power and what that means for the oppressed of the land.

One of the effective starting points for that encounter with reality is the body of black spirituals that came to maturity in the antebellum years. Far from being poignant expressions of shattered humanity, they were affirmations of hope—hope that enabled black slaves to risk their lives for earthly freedom because they knew they had a home "over yonder."

Black Theology on Revolution, Violence, and Reconciliation

1970

How is Christianity related to the black revolution in America? The answer to this question is not easy since we live in a white society that emphasizes the seeming discontinuity between "blackness-revolution" and the gospel of Jesus. Black consciousness as expressed in Black Power is by definition revolutionary in white America, if by revolution we mean a sudden, radical, and complete change; or as Jürgen Moltmann puts it: "a transformation in the foundations of a system—whether of economics, of politics, or morality, or of religion."[1] In America "law and order" means obedience to the law of white people, and "stability" means the continuation of the present in the light of the past—defined and limited by George Washington, Abraham Lincoln, and Richard Nixon. Revolution then means anything that challenges the "sacredness" of the past which is tantamount to usurping the rule of white oppressors. That is why J. Edgar Hoover described the Black Panthers as the most serious internal threat to the American way of life.

But for black people, revolution means that blacks no longer accept the history of white people as the key to their existence in the future. It also means they are prepared to do what is necessary in order to assure that their present and future existence will be defined by black visions of reality. We believe, as Ernst Bloch puts it: "Things can be otherwise. That means: things can also *become* otherwise: in the direction of evil, which must be avoided, or in the direction of good, which would have to be promoted."[2] The black revolution involves tension between the actual and the possible, the "white-past" and the "black-future," and the black community accepting the responsibility of defining the world according to its "open possibilities."

Moltmann is right: "Truth is revolutionary," that is, truth involves "discovering that the world can be changed and that nothing has to remain as

28

it has been."[3] White oppressors cannot share in this future reality as defined by the black revolution. Indeed, we blacks assume that the white position of unauthorized power as expressed in the racist character of every American institution—churches and seminaries not excluded!—renders white oppressors incapable of understanding what black humanity is, and it is thus incumbent upon us as black people to become "revolutionaries for blackness," rebelling against all who enslave us. With Marcus Garvey, we say: "Any sane man, race or nation that desires freedom must first of all think in terms of blood."

In contrast to the revolutionary thrust of Black Power, Christianity usually is not thought of as being involved in radical change. It has been identified with the status quo, a condition that encourages oppression and not human liberation. Some black religionists, like Howard Thurman and Albert Cleage, say that the Apostle Paul must bear a heavy responsibility for the theological justification of human oppression. It was Paul who admonished slaves to be obedient to their masters; in Romans 13, he urged all men to be subject to the state. While it is possible to question the use of Paul in this context, especially in view of the radical eschatological vision of first-century Christians and the contrasting differences between the social and political situation of Paul's time and ours, we cannot deny that later theologies used Paul as a theological justification of economic and political oppression. Indeed, it can be said that when Constantine made Christianity the official religion of the Roman State (replacing the public state sacrifices), the gospel of Jesus became a religious justification of the interests of the state. Theologians began to equate the immoral with the unlawful and slavery with the sins of the slaves. As Augustine put it: Slavery was due to the sinfulness of the slaves. Therefore, like Paul, he admonished "slaves to be subject to their masters . . ." serving them "with a good-heart and a good-will."[4]

During the Middle Ages, Thomas Aquinas took his cue from Augustine. "Slavery among men is natural," wrote Aquinas. "The slave, in regard to his master, is an instrument. . . . Between a master and his slave there is a special right of domination."[5]

The idea that the slave should be obedient to his master and should not seek to change his civil status through revolutionary violence is found throughout the Christian tradition. In Protestant Christianity, this emphasis is found in Martin Luther and his definition of the state as the servant of God. That was why he condemned the Peasants' revolt, saying that "nothing can be more poisonous, hurtful, or devilish than a rebel." He equated killing a rebel peasant with the killing of a mad dog.[6]

It is unfortunate that Protestant Christianity did not offer a serious challenge to modern slavery in Europe and America. Calvinism seemed especially suited for America with its easy affinity for capitalism and slavery. While John Wesley, the founder of Methodism, did not endorse slavery, he appeared to be more concerned about a warm heart than an enslaved body. And his evangelist friend George Whitefield publicly defended the slave institution in Georgia. It is a sad fact that Protestants not only tolerated slavery but frequently encouraged it.

The same emphasis is found in modern Catholicism. It rarely defended the interests of the oppressed. In 1903 Pope Pius X clarified the Catholic position:

> Human society as established by God is made up of unequal elements. . . . Accordingly, it is in conformity with the order of human society as established by God that there be rulers and ruled, employers and employees, learned and ignorant, nobles and plebeians.[7]

In 1943, in a similar vein, Pope Pius XII advised the Italian workers that

> [s]alvation and justice are not to be found in revolution but in evolution through concord. Violence has always achieved only destruction not construction; the kindling of passions, not their pacification; the accumulation of hate and ruin, not the reconciliation of the contending parties. And it has reduced men and parties to the difficult task of rebuilding, after sad experience, on the ruins of discord.[8]

We may conclude, then, that the essential differences between Protestants and Catholics do not lie in their stand on revolution. Both agree that the state has divine sanction and thus violent revolution must be condemned. And if there are rare exceptions in which violence can be justified, these exceptions do not apply to black people and their liberation struggle in America. In regard to the black revolution, Protestants and Catholics alike stand solidly on their tradition. It seems that the most "radical" comment coming from the white churches is: "We deplore the violence but sympathize with the reasons for the violence"—which is equivalent to saying "Of course we raped your women, dehumanized your men, and ghettoized the minds of your children, and you have a right to be upset, but that is no reason for you to burn our buildings. If you people keep acting like that, we will never give you your freedom."

Toward Liberation

Christians, unfortunately, are not known for their revolutionary actions. For the most part, the chief exponents of the Christian tradition have been identified primarily with the structures of power and only secondarily with the victims of power. This perhaps explains why white Christians in America tend to think of "love" as an absence of power and "reconciliation" as being indifferent to justice. It certainly accounts for the inauspicious distinction made between violence and force: "The state is invested with force; it is an organism instituted and ordained by God, and remains such even when it is unjust; even its harshest acts are not the same thing as the angry or brutal deed of the individual. The individual surrenders his passions, he commits violence."[9]

True, not all Christians have defended this perspective. The Left Wing tradition of the Protestant Reformation and the Quakers' stand on American slavery are possible exceptions. Prominent examples in our century are Reinhold Niebuhr's *Moral Man and Immoral Society*, the Confessing Church in Hitler's Germany, and particularly the noble example of Dietrich Bonhoeffer. We have already mentioned Jürgen Moltmann, and we could name other European theologians who are participating in the Marxist-Christian dialogue,[10] relating theology to revolutionary change. In America, Richard Shaull and Paul Lehmann have been defining the theological task according to the "politics of God," emphasizing the divine participation in the "messianic movements dedicated to the liberation of man from all that enslaves and dehumanizes him."[11]

But these examples are exceptions and not the rule. In America, at least, the Christian tradition is identified with the structures of racism in their oppression of black people. This was the reason for the white church's compliance with black slavery, its subsequent indifference toward oppression generally, and its failure to respond to the authentic demands of black reparations. No white theologian has taken the oppression of black people as a point of departure for analyzing the meaning of the gospel today. Apparently white theologians see no connection between blackness and the gospel of Jesus Christ. Even the so-called white American "theologians of revolution" did not receive their motivation from an identification with Black Americans but from Latin America, Vietnam, and other foreign lands. I do not want to minimize their theological endeavors or question the authenticity of their verbalized identification with the poor, "undeveloped" nations, but I believe, as Sartre puts it: "The only way of helping the enslaved out there is to take sides with those who are here."

What then is the answer to the question, "What relevance has Christian theology to the oppressed blacks of America?" Since whites have ignored this question, it is necessary to look beyond the white Christian tradition to the biblical tradition, investigating the latter in the light of the past and present manifestations of the black struggle for liberation.

Taking seriously the tradition of the Old and New Testaments and the past and present black revolution in America, *black* theology contends that the content of Christian theology is *liberation*. This means that theology is a rational and passionate study of the revolutionary activity of God in the world in the light of the historical situation of an oppressed community, relating the forces of liberation to the essence of the gospel, which is Jesus Christ. Theology so defined moves us in the direction of the biblical tradition which focuses on the activity of God in history, liberating people from human bondage. God, according to the Bible, is known by what he does, and what he does is always related to the liberation of the oppressed. This is the meaning of the saying:

> You have seen what I did to the Egyptians, and how I bore you on eagles' wings and brought you to myself. Now therefore, if you will obey my voice and keep my covenant, you shall be my own possession among all peoples. . . .
>
> *(Exod. 19:45a RSV)*

Here the Exodus is connected with the covenant, revealing that Israel's consciousness as the people of God is bound up with her escape from Egyptian slavery. Yahweh is the God of the oppressed and downtrodden and his revelation is made known *only* through the liberation of the oppressed. The covenant at Sinai, then, is not just a pious experience of God; it is a celebration of the God of liberation whose will is revealed in the freedom of slaves.

The equation of God's salvation with human liberation is found throughout biblical history, and particularly in God's incarnate appearance in Jesus Christ. By becoming the Oppressed One, God "made plain by this action that poverty, hunger, and sickness rob people of all dignity and that the Kingdom of God will fill them bodily with riches. The kingdom which Jesus preached and represented through his life is not only the soul's bliss but *shalom* for the body as well, peace on earth and liberation of the creature from the past."[12] This is the meaning of his birth in the stable at Bethlehem, his baptism with sinners, and his definition of his ministry for the poor, not the rich. God came to those who had no rights and "he celebrated the eschatological banquet."

> His resurrection from the humiliation of the cross can be understood as the revelation of the new creation of God's righteousness. In view of this, Christians are commissioned to bring . . . the justice of God and freedom into the world of oppression.[13]

With liberation as the essence of the Christian gospel, it becomes impossible to speak of the God of Hebrew history, the God who revealed himself in Jesus Christ, without recognizing that he is the God *of* and *for* those who labor and are heavy laden.

The emphasis on liberation not only leads us to the heart of the biblical message, it also enables theology to say something relevant to the black revolution in America. The liberation theme relates Black Power to the Christian gospel, and renders as an untruth the unverbalized white assumption that Christ is white, or that being Christian means that black people ought to turn the other cheek—as if we blacks have no moral right to defend ourselves from the encroachments of white people. To explicate the meaning of God's activity as revealed in the liberation of the oppressed blacks of America means that the theologian must lose his identity with the white structure and become unqualifiedly identified with the wretched of this land. It means that there can be no authentic Christian talk unless it focuses on the empowerment of the poor—defined and limited by their past, present, and future history. If God is truly the God of the weak and helpless, then we must critically reevaluate the history of theology in America, a theology that owes more to white oppressors than oppressed blacks or Indians. What about Gabriel Prosser, Denmark Vesey, and Nat Turner as theological sources for assessing the contemporary presence of Christ? Could it be that American theologians can best understand their task by studying LeRoi Jones, Malcolm X, or the Black Panthers rather than merely mouthing the recent rhetoric of German theologians? Hopefully, the rise of black theology will force American religionists to realize that no theology of the Christian gospel is possible that ignores the reality of the divine among black people in this country.

Violence as Curse and as Right

The black revolution involves a total break with the white past, "the overturning of relationships, the transformation of life, and then a reconstruction."[14] Theologically, this means that black people are prepared to live according to God's eschatological future as defined by the present reality of the black kingdom in the lives of oppressed people struggling for historical liberation. It is this perspective that informs black theology's reflections on the religious significance of the black revolution in America.

Because the black revolution means a radical break with the existing political and social structure and a redefinition of black life along the lines of black liberation, it is to be expected that white Christians and assorted moralists will ask questions about methods and means. Theologically and philosophically, they want to know whether revolutionary violence can be justified as an appropriate means for the attainment of black liberation. If black theology is Christian theology, how does it reconcile violence with Jesus' emphasis on love and reconciliation? Is it not true that violence is a negation of the gospel of Jesus Christ?

These are favorite *white* questions, and it is significant that they are almost always addressed to the oppressed and almost never to the oppressors. This fact alone provides the clue to the motive behind the questions. White people are not really concerned about violence per se but only when they are the victims. As long as blacks are beaten and shot, they are strangely silent, as if they are unaware of the inhumanity committed against the black community. Why did we not hear from the "nonviolent Christians" when black people were *violently* enslaved, *violently* lynched, and *violently* ghettoized in the name of freedom and democracy? When I hear questions about violence and love coming from the children of slavemasters whose identity with Jesus extends no further than that weekly Sunday service, then I can understand why many black brothers and sisters say that Christianity is the white man's religion, and that it must be destroyed along with white oppressors. What white people fail to realize is that their questions about violence and reconciliation not only are very

Might does not make right

naive, but are hypocritical and insulting. When whites ask me, "Are you for violence?" my rejoinder is: "Whose violence? Richard Nixon's or his victims'? The Mississippi State Police or the students at Jackson State? The Chicago Police or Fred Hampton?[15] What the hell are you talking about?" If we are going to raise the question of violence, it ought to be placed in its proper perspective.

(1) Violence is not only what black people do to white people as victims seek to change the structure of their existence; violence is what white people *did* when they created a society for white people only, and what they *do* in order to maintain it. Violence in America did not begin with the Black Power movement or with the Black Panther Party. Contrary to popular opinion, violence has a long history in America. This country was born in violent revolution (remember 1776?), and it has been sustained by the violent extermination of red people and the violent enslavement of black people. This is what Rap Brown had in mind when he said that "violence is American as cherry pie."

White people have a distorted conception of the meaning of violence. They like to think of violence as breaking the laws of their society, but that is a narrow and racist understanding of reality. There is a more deadly form of violence, and it is camouflaged in such slogans as "law and order," "freedom and democracy," and "the American way of life." I am speaking of white collar violence, the violence of Christian murderers and patriot citizens who define right in terms of whiteness and wrong as blackness. These are the people who hire assassins to do their dirty work while they piously congratulate themselves for being "good" and "nonviolent."

I contend, therefore, that the problem of violence is not the problem of a few black revolutionaries but the problem of a whole social structure which outwardly appears to be ordered and respectable but inwardly is "ridden by psychopathic obsessions and delusions"[16]—racism and hate. Violence is embedded in American law, and it is blessed by the keepers of moral sanctity. This is the core of the problem of violence, and it will not be solved by romanticizing American history, pretending that Hiroshima, Nagasaki, and Vietnam are the first American crimes against humanity. If we take seriously the idea of human dignity, then we know that the annihilation of Indians, the enslavement of blacks, and the making of heroes out of slaveholders, like George Washington and Thomas Jefferson, were America's first crimes against humankind. And it does not help the matter at all to attribute black slavery to economic necessity or an accident of history. America is an unjust society and black people have known that for a long time.

(2) If violence is not just a question for the oppressed but *primarily* for the oppressors, then it is obvious that the distinction between violence and nonviolence is false and misleading. "The problem of violence and nonviolence is an illusory problem. There is only the question of the justified and unjustified use of force and the question of whether the means are proportionate to the ends";[17] and the only people who can answer that problem are the victims of injustice.

Concretely, ours is a situation in which the only option we have is that of deciding whose violence we will support—the oppressors or the oppressed, whites or blacks. Either we side with oppressed blacks and other unwanted minorities as they try to redefine the meaning of their existence in a dehumanized society, or we take a stand with the American government whose interests have been expressed in police clubs and night sticks, tear gas and machine guns. There is no possibility of neutrality—the moral luxury of being on neither side. Neither the government nor black people will allow that! The government demands support through taxes, the draft, and public allegiance to the American flag. Black people demand that you deny whiteness as an appropriate form of human existence, and that you be willing to take the risk to create a new humanity. With Franz Fanon, we do not believe it wise to leave our destiny to Europeans. "We must invent and we must make discoveries. . . . For Europe, for ourselves, and for humanity . . . we must turn over a new leaf, we must work out new concepts, and try to set afoot a new man."[18]

(3) If violence versus nonviolence is not the issue but rather the creation of a new humanity, then the critical question for Christians is not whether Jesus committed violence or whether violence is theoretically consistent with love and reconciliation. The question is not what Jesus *did*, as if his behavior in the first century is the infallible ethical guide for our actions today. We must ask not what he did but what he is *doing*, and what he did becomes important only insofar as it points to his activity today. To use the Jesus of history as an absolute ethical guide for people today is to become enslaved to the past, foreclosing God's eschatological future and its judgment on the present. It removes the element of risk in ethical decisions and makes people slaves to principles. But the gospel of "Jesus means freedom"[19] (as Ernst Käsemann has put it), and one essential element of that freedom is the existential burden of making decisions about human

liberation without being completely sure what Jesus did or would do. *This is the risk of faith.*

My difficulty with white theologians is their use of Jesus' so-called non-violent attitude in the Gospels as the primary evidence that black people ought to be nonviolent today. Not only have Rudolf Bultmann and other form critics demonstrated that there are historical difficulties in the attempt to move behind the kerygmatic preaching of the early church to the real Jesus of Nazareth, but, moreover, the resurrected Christ is not bound by first-century possibilities. Therefore it is possible to conclude that the man from Nazareth was not a revolutionary zealot, and still contend that the risen Christ is involved in the black revolution today. Though the Jesus of yesterday is important for our ethical decisions today, we must be careful where we locate that importance. It is not to be found in following in his steps, slavishly imitating his behavior in Palestine. Rather we must regard his past activity as a *pointer* to what he is doing now. It is not so much what he did; but his actions were signs of God's eschatological future and his will to liberate all people from slavery and oppression. To be for Jesus means being for the oppressed and unwanted in human society.

As Christians, we are commanded not to follow principles but to discover the will of God in a troubled and dehumanized world. Concretely, we must decide not between good and evil or right and wrong, but between the oppressors and the oppressed, whites and blacks. We must ask and answer the question, "Whose actions are consistent with God's work in history?" Either we believe that God's will is revealed in the status quo of America or in the actions of those who seek to change it.

Accepting the risk of faith and the ethical burden of making decisions about life and death without an infallible guide, black theology contends that God is found among the poor, the wretched, and the sick. "God chose what is foolish in the world to shame the wise [wrote Paul], God chose what is weak in the world to shame the strong, God chose what is low and despised in the world, even the things that are not, to bring to nothing things that are . . ." (1 Cor. 1:26f.). That was why God elected Israelite slaves and not Egyptian slavemasters—the weak and the poor in Israel, not the oppressors. As Jesus' earthly life demonstrated, the God of Israel is a God whose will is made known through his identification with the oppressed and whose activity is always identical with those who strive for a liberated freedom.

If this message means anything for our times, it means that God's revelation is found in black liberation. God has chosen what is black in America to shame the whites. In a society where white is equated with good and black is defined as bad, humanity and divinity mean an unqualified identification with blackness. The divine election of the oppressed means that black people are given the power of judgment over the high and mighty whites.

Two Kinds of Reconciliation?

When black theology emphasizes the right of black people to defend themselves against those who seek to destroy them, it never fails that white people then ask, "What about the biblical doctrine of reconciliation?" Whites who ask that question should not be surprised if blacks respond, "Yeah man, what about it?" The difficulty is not with the reconciliation question per se but with the people asking it. Like the question of violence, this question is almost always addressed *to* blacks *by* whites, as if we blacks are responsible for the demarcation of community on the basis of color. They who are responsible for the dividing walls of hostility, racism, and hate want to know whether the victims are ready to forgive and forget—without changing the balance of power. They want to know whether we have any hard feelings toward them, whether we still love them, even though we are oppressed and brutalized by them. What can we say to people who insist on oppressing black people but get upset when black people reject them?

Because black liberation is the point of departure of black theology's analysis of the gospel of Jesus, it cannot accept a view of reconciliation based on white values. The Christian view of reconciliation has nothing to do with black people being nice to white people as if the gospel demands that we ignore their insults and their humiliating presence. It does not mean discussing with whites what it means to be black or going to white gatherings and displaying what whites call an understanding attitude—remaining cool and calm amid racists and bigots.

To understand the Christian view of reconciliation and its relation to black liberation, it is necessary to focus on the Bible. Here reconciliation is connected with divine liberation. According to the Bible, reconciliation is what God does for enslaved people who are unable to break the chains of slavery. To be reconciled is to be set free; it is to have the chains struck off the body and mind so that the creatures of God can be what they are. Reconciliation means that people cannot be human and God cannot be God unless the creatures of God are liberated from that which enslaves and is dehumanizing.

When Paul says, "God was in Christ reconciling the world unto himself," this is not a sentimental comment on race relations. The reconciling act of God in Christ is centered on the cross, and it reveals the extent that God is willing to go in order to set people free from slavery and oppression. The cross means that the Creator has taken upon himself all human pain and suffering, revealing that God cannot be unless oppression ceases to be. Through the death and resurrection of Christ, God places the oppressed in a new state of humanity, now free to live according to God's intentions for humanity.

Because God has set us free, we are now commanded to go and be reconciled with our neighbors, and particularly our white neighbors. But this does not mean letting whites define the terms of reconciliation. It means participating in God's revolutionizing activity in the world, changing the political, economic, and social structures so that distinctions between rich and poor, oppressed and oppressors, are no longer a reality. To be reconciled with white people means destroying their oppressive power, reducing them to the human level and thereby putting them on equal footing with other humans. There can be no reconciliation with masters as long as they are masters, as long as men are in prison. There can be no communication between masters and slaves until masters no longer exist, are no longer present as masters. The Christian task is to rebel against all masters, destroying their pretensions to authority and ridiculing the symbols of power.

However, it must be remembered that oppressors never take kindly to those who question their authority. They do not like "thugs and bums," people who disregard their power, and they will try to silence them any way they can. But if we believe that our humanity transcends them and is not dependent on their goodwill, then we can fight against them even though it may mean death.

Black Theology and the Black Church:
Where Do We Go from Here?

Since the appearance of black theology in the late 1960s, much has been written and said about the political involvement of the Black Church in black people's historical struggle for justice in North America. Black theologians and preachers have rejected the white church's attempt to separate love from justice and religion from politics because we are proud descendents of a black religious tradition that has always interpreted its confession of faith according to the people's commitment to the struggle for earthly freedom. Instead of turning to Reinhold Niebuhr and John Bennett for ethical guidance in those troubled times, we searched our past for insight, strength, and the courage to speak and do the truth in an extreme situation of oppression. Richard Allen, James Varick, Harriet Tubman, Sojourner Truth, Henry McNeal Turner, and Martin Luther King, Jr., became household names as we attempted to create new theological categories that would express our historical fight for justice.

It was in this context that the "Black Power" statement was written in July 1966 by an ad hoc National Committee of Negro Churchmen.[1] The cry of Black Power by Willie Ricks and its political and intellectual development by Stokely Carmichael and others challenged the Black Church to move beyond the models of love defined in the context of white religion and theology. The Black Church was thus faced with a theological dilemma: Either reject Black Power as a contradiction of Christian love (and thereby join the white church in its condemnation of Black Power advocates as un-American and unchristian), or accept Black Power as a sociopolitical expression of the truth of the gospel. These two possibilities were the only genuine alternatives before us, and we had to decide on whose side we would take our stand.

We knew that to define Black Power as the opposite of the Christian faith was to reject the central role that the Black Church has played in black people's historical struggle for freedom. Rejecting Black Power also meant that the Black Church would ignore its political responsibility to empower black people in their present struggle to make our children's future more humane than intended by the rulers in this society. Faced with these unavoidable consequences, it was not possible for any self-respecting churchperson to desecrate the memories of our mothers and fathers in the faith by siding with white people who murdered and imprisoned black people simply because of our persistent audacity to assert our freedom. To side with white theologians and preachers who questioned the theological legitimacy of Black Power would have been similar to siding with St. George Methodist Church against Richard Allen and the Bethelites in their struggle for independence during the late eighteenth and early nineteenth centuries. We knew that we could not do that, and no amount of white theological reasoning would be allowed to blur our vision of the truth.

But to accept the second alternative and thereby locate Black Power in the Christian context was not easy. First, the acceptance of Black Power would appear to separate us from Martin Luther King, Jr., and we did not want to do that. King was our model, having creatively combined religion and politics, and black preachers and theologians respected his courage to concretize the political consequences of his confession of faith. Thus we hesitated to endorse the "Black Power" movement, since it was created in the context of the James Meredith March by Carmichael and others in order to express their dissatisfaction with King's continued emphasis on nonviolence and Christian love.[2] As a result of this sharp confrontation between Carmichael and King, black theologians and preachers felt themselves caught in a terrible predicament of wanting to express their continued respect for and solidarity with King, but disagreeing with this rejection of Black Power.

Secondly, the concept of Black Power presented a problem for black theologians and preachers not only because of our loyalty to Martin Luther King, but also because many of us had been trained in white seminaries and had internalized much of white people's definition of Christianity. While the rise and growth of independent black churches suggested that black people had a different perception of the gospel than whites, there was no formal theological tradition to which we could turn in order to justify our definition of Black Power as an expression of the Christian gospel. But if we intended to fight on a theological and intellectual level as a way of empowering our historical and political struggle for justice, we had to create a new theological movement, one that was derived from and thus accountable to our people's fight for justice. To accept Black Power as Christian required that we thrust ourselves into our history in order to search for new ways to think and be black in this world. We felt the need to explain ourselves and to be understood from our own vantage point and not from the perspective and experiences of whites. When white liberals questioned this approach to theology, our response was very similar to the bluesman in Mississippi when told he was not singing his song correctly: "Look-a-heah, man, dis yere *mah song*, en I'll sing it howsoevah I pleases."[3]

Thus we sang our Black Power songs, knowing that the white church establishment would not smile upon our endeavors to define Christianity independently of their own definitions of the gospel. For the power of definition is a prerogative that oppressors never want to give up. Furthermore, to *say* that love is compatible with Black Power is one thing, but to demonstrate this compatibility in theology and the praxis of life is another. If the reality of a thing was no more than its verbalization in a written document, the Black Church since 1966 would be a model of the creative integration of theology and life, faith and the struggle for justice. But we know that the meaning of reality is found *only* in its historical embodiment in people as structured in societal arrangements. Love's meaning is not found in sermons or theological textbooks but rather in the creation of social structures that are not dehumanizing and oppressive. This insight impressed itself on our religious consciousness, and we were deeply troubled by the inadequacy of our historical obedience when measured by our faith claims. From 1966 to the present, black theologians and preachers, both in the church and on the streets, have been searching for new ways to confess and to live our faith in God so that the Black Church would not make religion the opiate of our people.

The term *black theology* was created in this social and religious context. It was initially understood as the theological arm of Black Power, and it enabled us to express our theological imagination in the struggle of freedom independently of white theologians. It was the one term that white ministers and theologians did not like, because, like Black Power in politics, black theology located the theological starting point in the black experience and not the particularity of the Western theological tradition. We did not feel ourselves accountable to Aquinas, Luther, or Calvin but to David Walker, Daniel Payne, and W. E. B. Du Bois. The depth and passion in which we expressed our solidarity with the black experience over against the Western tradition led some black scholars in religion to reject theology itself as alien to the black culture.[4] Others, while not rejecting theology entirely, contended that black theologians should turn primarily to African religion and philosophy in order to develop a black theology consistent with and accountable to our historical roots.[5] But all of us agreed that we were living at the beginning of a new historical moment, and this required the development of a *black* frame of reference that many called "black theology."

The consequence of our affirmation of a black theology led to the creation of black caucuses in white churches, a permanent ecumenical church body under the title of the National Conference of Black Churchmen (NCBC), and the endorsement of James Forman's "Black Manifesto." In June 1969 at the Interdenominational Theological Center in Atlanta and under the aegis of NCBC's Theological Commission, a group of black theologians met to write a policy statement on black theology. This statement, influenced by my book *Black Theology and Black Power*, which had appeared two months earlier, defined black theology as a "theology of black liberation."[6]

Black theology, then, was not created in a vacuum and neither was it simply the intellectual enterprise of black professional theologians. Like our sermons and songs, black theology was born in the context of the black community as black people were attempting to make sense out of their struggle for freedom. In one sense, black theology is as old as when the first African refused to accept slavery as consistent with religion and as recent as when a black person intuitively recognizes that the confession of the Christian faith receives its meaning only in relation to political justice. Although black theology may be considered to have formally appeared only when the first book was published on it in 1969, informally, the reality that made the book possible was already present in the black experience and was found in our songs, prayers, and sermons. In these outpourings are expressed the black visions of truth, preeminently the certainty that we were created not for slavery but for freedom. Without this dream of freedom, so vividly expressed in the life, teachings, and death of Jesus, Malcolm, and Martin, there would be no black theology, and we would have no reason to be assembled in this place. We have come here today to plan our future and to map out our strategy because we have a dream that has not been realized.

To be sure, we have talked and written about this dream. Indeed, every Sunday morning black people gather in our churches to find out where we are in relation to the actualization of our dream. The Black Church community really believes that where there is no vision the people perish. If people have no dreams they will accept the world as it is and will not seek to change it. To dream is to know what is ain't supposed to be.

What visions do we have for the people today? Do we still believe with Martin King that "we as a people will get to the promised land"? If so, how will we get there? Will we get there simply by preaching sermons and singing songs about it? What is the Black Church doing to actualize the dreams it talks about? These are hard questions, and they are not intended as a put-down of the Black Church. I was born in the Black Church in Bearden, Arkansas, and began my ministry in that church at the early age of sixteen. Everything I am as well as what I know that I ought to be was shaped in the context of the Black Church. Indeed, it is because I love the church that I am required, as one of its theologians and preachers, to ask, "When does the Black Church's actions deny its faith? What are the activities in our churches that should be not only rejected as unchristian but also exposed as demonic? What are the evils in our church and community that we should commit ourselves to destroy?" Bishops, pastors, and church executives do not like to disclose the wrongdoings of their respective denominations. They are like doctors, lawyers, and other professionals who seem bound to keep silent, because to speak the truth is to guarantee one's exclusion from the inner dynamics of power in the profession. But I contend that the *faith* of the Black Church lays a claim upon all churchpeople that transcends the social mores of a given profession. Therefore, to cover up and to minimize the sins of the church is to guarantee its destruction as a community of faith, committed to the liberation of the oppressed. If we want the Black Church to live beyond our brief histories and thus to serve as the "Old Ship of Zion" that will carry the people home to freedom, then we had better examine the direction in which the ship is going. Who is the Captain of the Ship, and what are his economic and political interests? This question should not only be applied to bishops, but to pastors and theologians, deacons and stewards. Unless we are willing to apply the most severe scientific analysis to our church communities in terms of economics and politics and are willing to confess and repent of our sins in the struggle for liberation, then the Black Church, as we talk about it, will remain a relic of history and nothing more. God will have to raise up new instruments of freedom so that his faithfulness to liberate the poor and weak can be realized in history. We must not forget that God's Spirit will use us as her instrument only insofar as we remain agents of liberation by using our resources for the empowerment of the poor and weak. But if we, like Israel in the Old Testament, forget about our Exodus experience and the political responsibility it lays upon us to be the historical embodiment of freedom, then, again like Israel, we will become objects of God's judgment. It is very easy for us to expose the demonic and oppressive character of the white church, and I have done my share of that. But such exposures of the sins of the white church, without applying the same criticism to ourselves, is hypocritical and serves as a camouflage of our own shortcomings and sins. Either we mean what we say about liberation or we do not. If we mean it, the time has come for an inventory in terms of the authenticity of our faith as defined by the historical commitment of the black denominational churches to liberation.

Yes in every paradigm

I have lectured and preached about the Black Church's involvement in our liberation struggle all over North America. I have told the stories of Richard Allen and James Varick, Adam Clayton Powell and Martin Luther King. I have talked about the double-meaning in the Spirituals, the passion of the sermon and prayer, the ecstasy of the shout and conversion experience in terms of an eschatological happening in the lives of people, empowering them to fight for earthly freedom. Black theology, I have contended, is a theology of liberation, because it has emerged out of and is accountable to a Black Church that has always been involved in our historical fight for justice. When black preachers and laypeople hear this message, they respond enthusiastically and with a sense of pride that they belong to a radical and creative tradition. But when I speak to young blacks in colleges and universities, most are surprised that such a radical Black Church tradition really exists. After hearing about David Walker's "Appeal" in 1829, Henry H. Garnet's "Address to the Slaves" in 1843, and Henry M. Turner's affirmation that "God is a Negro" in 1898, these young blacks are shocked. Invariably they ask, "Whatever happened to the black churches of today? Why don't we have the same radical spirit in our preachers and churches?" Young blacks contend that the black churches of today, with very few exceptions, are not involved in liberation but primarily concerned with how much money they raise for a new church building or the preacher's anniversary.

This critique of the Black Church is not limited to young college students. Many black people view the church as a hindrance to black liberation, because black preachers and church members appear to be more concerned about their own institutional survival than the freedom of the poor people in their communities. "Historically," many radical blacks say, "the Black Church was involved in the struggle but today it is not." They often turn the question back upon me: "All right, granted what you say about the historical Black Church, but *where* is an institutional Black Church denomination that still embodies the vision that brought it into existence? Are you saying that the present-day A.M.E. Church or A.M.E. Zion Church has the same historical commitment for justice that it had under the leadership of Allen and Payne or Rush and Varick?" Sensing they have a point difficult to refute, these radicals then say it is not only impossible to find a Black Church denomination committed to black liberation but also difficult to find a local congregation that defines its ministry in terms of the needs of the oppressed and their liberation.

Whatever we might think about the unfairness of this severe indictment, we would be foolish to ignore it. For connected with this black critique is our international image. In the African context, not to mention Asia and Latin America, the Black Church experiences a similar credibility problem. There is little in our theological expressions and church practice that rejects American capitalism or recognizes its oppressive character in Third World countries. The time has come for us to move beyond institutional survival in a capitalistic and racist society and begin to take more seriously our dreams about a new heaven and a new earth. Does this dream include capitalism or is it a radically new way of life more consistent with African socialism as expressed in the *Arusha Declaration* in Tanzania?[7]

Black theologians and churchpeople must now move beyond a mere reaction to white racism in America and begin to extend our vision of a new socially constructed humanity for the whole inhabited world. We must be concerned with the quality of human life not only in the ghettos of American cities but also in Africa, Asia, and Latin America. Since humanity is one, and cannot be isolated into racial and national groups, there will be no freedom for anyone until there is freedom for all. This means that we must enlarge our vision by connecting it with that of other oppressed peoples so that together all the victims of the world might take charge of their history for the creation of a new humanity. As Franz Fanon taught us, if we wish to live up to our people's expectations, we must look beyond European and American capitalism.

New times require new concepts and methods. To dream is not enough. We must come down from the mountaintop and experience the hurts and pain of the people in the valley. Our dreams need to be socially analyzed, for without scientific analysis they will vanish into the night. Furthermore, social analysis will test the nature of our commitment to the dreams we preach and sing about. This is one of the important principles we learned from Martin King and many black preachers who worked with him. Real substantial change in societal structures requires scientific analysis. King's commitment to social analysis not only characterized his involvement in the Civil Rights movement but also led him to take a radical stand against the war in Vietnam. Through scientific analysis, King saw the connection between the oppression of blacks in the U.S. and America's involvement in Vietnam. It is to his credit that he never allowed a pietistic faith in the other world to become a substitute for good judgment in this world. He not only preached sermons about the promised land but concretized his vision with a political attempt to actualize his hope.

I realize, with Merleau-Ponty, that "one does not become a revolutionary through science but through indignation."[8] Every revolution needs its Rosa Parks. This point has often been overlooked by Marxists and other sociologists who seem to think that all answers are found in scientific analysis. Mao Tse-tung responded to such an attitude with this comment: "There are people who think that Marxism is a kind of magic truth with which one can cure any disease. We should tell them that dogmas are more useless than cow dung. Dung can be used as fertilizer."[9]

But these comments do not disprove the truth of the Marxists' social analysis which focuses on economics and class and is intended as empowerment for the oppressed to radically change human social arrangements. Such an analysis will help us to understand the relation between economics and oppression not only in North America but throughout the world. Liberation is not a process limited to black-white relations in the United States; it is also something to be applied to the relations between rich and poor nations. If we are an African people, as some of the names of our churches suggest, in what way are we to understand the political meaning of that identity? In what way does the economic investment of our church resources reflect our commitment to Africa and other oppressed people in the world? For if an economic analysis of our material resources does not reveal our commitment to the process of liberation, how can we claim that the Black Church and its theology are concerned about the freedom of oppressed peoples? As an Argentine peasant poet said:

> They say that God cares for the poor
> Well this may be true or not,
> But I know for a fact
> That he dines with the mine-owner.[10]

Because the Christian Church has supported the capitalists, many Marxists contend that "all revolutions have clashed with Christianity because *historically* Christianity has been structurally counter-revolutionary."[11] We may rightly question this assertion and appeal to the revolutionary expressions of Christianity in the black religious tradition, from Nat Turner to Martin Luther King. My concern, however, is not to debate the fine points of what constitutes revolution, but to open up the reality of the Black Church experience and its revolutionary potential to a world context. This means that we can learn from people in Africa, Asia, and Latin America, and they can learn from us. Learning from others involves listening to creative criticism; to exclude such criticism is to isolate ourselves from world politics, and this exclusion makes our faith nothing but a reflection of our economic interests. If Jesus Christ is more than a religious expression of our economic and sexist interests, then there is no reason to resist the truth of the Marxist and feminist analyses.

I contend that black theology is not afraid of truth from any quarter. We simply reject the attempt of others to tell us what truth is without our participation in its definition. That is why dogmatic Marxists seldom succeed in the black community, especially when the dogma is filtered through a brand of white racism not unlike that of the capitalists. If our long history of struggle has taught us anything, it is that if we are to be free, we black people will have to do it. *Freedom is not a gift but is a risk that must be taken.* No one can tell us what liberation is and how we ought to struggle for it, as if liberation can be found in words. Liberation is a process to be located and understood only in an oppressed community struggling for freedom. If there are people in and outside our community who want to talk to us about this liberation process in global terms and from Marxist and other perspectives, we should be ready to talk. But *only* if they are prepared to listen to us and we to them will genuine dialogue take place. For I will not listen to anybody who refuses to take racism seriously, especially when they themselves have not been victims of it. And they should listen to us *only* if we are prepared to listen to them in terms of the particularity of oppression in their historical context.

Therefore, I reject dogmatic Marxism that reduces every contradiction to class analysis and thus ignores racism as a legitimate point of departure in the process of liberation. There are racist Marxists as there are racist capitalists, and we must struggle against both. But we must be careful not to reject the Marxist's social analysis simply because we do not like the vessels that the message comes in. If we do that, then it is hard to explain how we can remain Christians in view of the white vessels in which the gospel was first introduced to black people.

The world is small. Both politically and economically, our freedom is connected with the struggles of oppressed peoples throughout the world. This is the truth of Pan-Africanism as represented in the life and thought of W. E. B. Du Bois, George Padmore, and C. L. R. James. Liberation knows no color bar; the very nature of the gospel is universalism, that is, a liberation that embraces the whole of humanity.

The need for a global perspective, which takes seriously the struggles of oppressed peoples in other parts of the world, has already been recognized in black theology, and small beginnings have been made with conferences on African and black theologies in Tanzania, New York, and Ghana. Another example of the recognition of this need is reflected in the dialogue on black theology between South Africa and North America. From the very beginning black theology has been influenced by a world perspective as defined by Henry M. Turner, Marcus Garvey, and the Pan-Africanism inaugurated in the life and work of W. E. B. Du Bois. The importance of this Pan-African perspective in black religion and theology has been cogently defended in Gayraud Wilmore's *Black Religion and Black Radicalism*. Our active involvement in the "Theology in the Americas," under whose aegis this conference is held, is an attempt to enlarge our perspective in relation to Africa, Asia, and Latin America as well as to express our solidarity with other oppressed minorities in the U.S.

This global perspective in black theology enlarges our vision regarding the process of liberation. What does black theology have to say about the fact that two-thirds of humanity is poor and that this poverty arises from the exploitation of the poor nations by rich nations? The people of the U.S.

compose 6 percent of the world's population, but we consume 40 percent of the world's resources. What, then, is the implication of the black demand for justice in the U.S. when related to justice for all the world's victims? Of the dependent status we experience in relation to white people, and the experience of Third World countries in relation to the U.S.? Thus, in our attempt to liberate ourselves from white America in the U.S., it is important to be sensitive to the complexity of the world situation and the oppressive role of the U.S. in it. African, Latin American, and Asian theologians, sociologists, and political scientists can aid us in the analysis of this complexity. In this analysis, our starting point in terms of racism is not negated but enhanced when connected with imperialism and sexism.

We must create a global vision of human liberation and include in it the distinctive contribution of the black experience. We have been struggling for nearly 400 years! What has that experience taught us that would be useful in the creation of a new historical future for all oppressed peoples? And what can others teach us from their historical experience in the struggle for justice? This is the issue that black theology needs to address. "Theology in the Americas" provides a framework in which to address it. I hope that we will not back off from this important task but face it with courage, knowing that the future of humanity is in the hands of oppressed peoples, because God has said, "Those who hope in me shall not be put to shame" (Isa. 49:23).

Martin and Malcolm

1998

Although Martin King was a Christian preacher of the black Baptist tradition and Malcolm X was a minister in the religion of Islam, the distinguishing mark of their thought and practice was their commitment to justice for the poor and their willingness to die for it.

—*For My People: Black Theology and the Black Church,* 1984

Martin King belongs to *all* Americans (blacks, whites, Asians, Hispanics, and Native peoples) who are struggling for justice and peace in this society. He represents what this land should mean for all its inhabitants, namely, a place in which the dignity of everyone is recognized and respected.

Union Seminary Quarterly Review, 1986

The Theology of
Martin Luther King, Jr.

Centuries ago Jeremiah raised a question, "Is there no balm in Gilead? Is there no physician?" He raised it because he saw the good people suffering so often and the evil people prospering. Centuries later our slave foreparents came along and they too saw the injustices of life and had nothing to look forward to morning after morning but the rawhide whip of the overseer, long rows of cotton and the sizzling heat, but they did an amazing thing. They looked back across the centuries and they took Jeremiah's question mark and straightened it into an exclamation point. And they could sing, "There is a balm in Gilead to make the wounded whole. There is a balm in Gilead to heal the sin-sick soul."[1]

It seems clear that the major obstacle in viewing Martin Luther King, Jr., as a creative theologian (and one of the most important in American history) is the narrow, elitist, and racist definition of theology that limits its methods and subject matter to problems that whites identify. If by contrast one insists that the struggle for freedom is the only appropriate context for doing theology, then King's importance as a theologian can be appreciated.

King was no armchair theologian. He was a theologian of action, an engaged theologian, actively seeking to transform the structures of oppression. His thinking emerged from his efforts to establish a just society. Therefore, it is possible to analyze his thought only in connection with such events as the successful Montgomery bus boycott (1955–56), his defeat in Albany (1961), the Birmingham demonstrations (1963), the Selma March for voting rights (1965), his encounter with racism in Chicago (1966), his dialogue with Black Power advocates during and after the Meredith, Mississippi, March (1966), his preparation for the Poor People's

March on Washington (1967), his stand against the Vietnam War (1967–68), and his last march with garbage workers in Memphis (1968). In each of these crises, King refined his theology according to the needs of the people with whom and for whom he was struggling. His theology was not permanent or static but was dynamic, constantly emerging from the historical circumstances in which he was engaged.

King's theology focused on the themes of justice, love, and hope, all grounded in the Black Church's faith in Jesus Christ. In addition to the Black Church tradition, King drew from other intellectual sources, namely, black "secular" integrationism, Protestant liberalism, and the nonviolent protest tradition of Gandhi and Thoreau. From these four sources, King created a coherent theology in the midst of the freedom struggle. The first part of this essay consists of an examination of the four sources and their contributions, including the themes of justice, love, and hope. The second part examines the function and interrelationship of the sources. The third part shows the development of King's thought from 1955 to 1968. I will conclude with a brief assessment of King's importance as an American theologian.

The Sources of King's Theology

The Black Integrationist Tradition

It is important to recognize that there has been a black integrationist tradition in this country for a century and a half, related to the Black Church but often at odds with it. It was founded in the black abolitionism of Frederick Douglass and redefined for this century in the protest of W. E. B. Du Bois and his allies against Booker T. Washington's accommodationism. It was institutionalized in the NAACP and the National Urban League. This line of black thought precedes by decades the Social Gospel movement within liberal Protestantism, which in any case seldom included the liberation of blacks in its agenda.

No one embodied in his life and thought the central ideas of the integrationist tradition more clearly than did Martin Luther King, Jr. No one proclaimed the vision of an integrated society with the oratorical power comparable to his sermons and speeches. In this regard, his greatest moment was his "I Have a Dream" address in Washington in 1963. King gave many versions of this speech before and after the Washington address, because his idea of the "American Dream" was the political symbol for his theological claims about the "beloved community." While Walter Rauschenbusch and other liberal theologians influenced his views regarding the American dream and the beloved community, the integration tradition of Douglass, NAACP, and the Urban League was more decisive in determining King's ideas.

The integrationist tradition shared the political optimism of Protestant liberalism and, even more than the latter, embraced the values of the American democratic tradition as embodied in the Declaration of Independence and the Constitution, providing a bridge for King's approach to white America. Furthermore, integrationist thought resonated with the Black Church tradition, particularly in its sense of hope and the worth of the human personality, leading many blacks to see King as the prophet of a new day.

Protestant Liberalism

This tradition made far less impact on King's thought than most of his interpreters have claimed and than King himself suggested.[2] Nevertheless, it contributed significantly to the process of his intellectual development. First, liberalism showed King how to deal with elements of naive conservatism in the Black Church that had repelled him even as a child. Liberal theology rejected both rigid orthodoxy and modern humanism, each of which emerged in response to the secular spirit of the eighteenth century Enlightenment, largely defined by the rise of scientific thinking. Liberal theologians who influenced King included Walter Rauschenbusch, George Davis, and L. Harold DeWolf. They applied the critical spirit of rational reflection to theology and the Bible and insisted upon the reasonableness of the Christian faith. They rejected almost everything that the fundamentalist and orthodox theologians were affirming as essentials of the faith: the inerrancy of the Bible, virgin birth of Jesus, substitutionary theory of atonement, bodily resurrection of Jesus, miracles, and similar creedal formulations.

Secondly, liberal thinkers introduced King to Hegel's dialectical method of analyzing history. King went to Boston University to study with Edgar S. Brightman, who guided him in a serious study of Hegel. After Brightman's untimely death during King's first year of graduate study, King continued his study of Hegel under the direction of Peter A. Bertocci and L. Harold

DeWolf. King said of Hegel: "His contention that 'truth is the whole' led me to a philosophical method of rational coherence. His analysis of the dialectical process . . . helped me to see that growth comes through struggle."[3] It also gave his own theology a dialectical quality. King's thought, like Hegel's, emerged out of his encounter with two opposites and his endeavor to achieve a synthesis of the truth found in each. For example, King's philosophy of integration and his strategy of nonviolent direct action were developed out of his rejection of both the accommodationism of black conservatives and the separatism of black nationalists. Black conservatives failed to realize that passivity in response to injustice merely contributes to its continued existence. Black nationalists failed to realize that a just community cannot be created in an atmosphere of hate and violence. A just community is an integrated community, black and white together, and it can be created only through nonviolence (love) and not violence (hate). Jesus and Gandhi provided a synthesis that moved beyond two opposites—powerless love and loveless power. Robert Penn Warren correctly said of King that "his philosophy is a way of living with intense polarity."[4]

Thirdly, liberalism showed him, as the classical integrationists could not, a rationale for relating religion to social change. King found his own concern for ethics and justice present in liberal theology, especially that of Walter Rauschenbusch. There is no doubt that Rauschenbusch's *Christianity and the Social Crisis* (1907) made a profound impact on Martin King's theology, particularly Rauschenbusch's interpretation of the message of the Hebrew prophets and the "social aims of Jesus."[5] King's admiration of Brightman grew from an appreciation of the ethical implications of Brightman's philosophy of personalism. "It [personalism]," said King, "gave me metaphysical and philosophical grounding for the idea of a personal God, and it gave me a metaphysical basis for the dignity and worth of all human personality."[6]

King shared the liberals' rejection of the neo-orthodox theology of the middle decades of this century. Though he probably did not study Barth seriously, he regarded Barth as anti-rational and semi-fundamentalist.[7] To be sure, King read Reinhold Niebuhr and was deeply influenced by his *Moral Man and Immoral Society* (1932), especially Niebuhr's analysis of the self-interested orientation of groups when compared to individuals. He was also deeply moved by Niebuhr's critique of pacifism. Nevertheless, King felt that Niebuhr's estimate of human nature was too low and his view of love was restricted to relations between individuals and not applicable to society.[8]

In his essay entitled "Pilgrimage to Nonviolence," King analyzes the impact of liberal theology upon his thinking. The influence of liberal theology can be seen clearly in many of the major emphases of his theology: optimism regarding human nature, accent on the beloved community, love as the central meaning of the gospel, the "unique God-consciousness of Jesus," the value of human personality, ethical activity as a necessary corollary of the Christian faith, God's imminent presence in the world —all of these ideas are prominently present in liberal Protestant thought.

Mohandas K. Gandhi and Henry David Thoreau

Though liberal theology influenced King's philosophical understanding of love, it was the philosophy of Mahatma Gandhi, the "little brown man" from India, as King called him, who provided the intellectual justification and the methodological implementation of his perspective on nonviolent direct action. Thoreau provided the philosophical justification for civil disobedience in the context of the North American democratic tradition. Martin King was introduced to Thoreau's *Civil Disobedience* during his student days at Morehouse and to the importance of Gandhi as a student at Crozer Seminary and, in a special way, at a lecture by Mordecai Johnson during the same period. Under the influence of Bayard Rustin and Glen Smiley, King became a firm devotee of Gandhi's theory of nonviolence. He connected Gandhi with Jesus and began to see his philosophy of nonviolence as similar to Jesus' suffering love on the cross. The idea that "unmerited suffering is redemptive" emerged as a dominant theme in King's theology as he constantly reminded blacks that they would experience a "season of suffering" before justice is achieved.[9]

The centrality of Gandhi and Jesus, nonviolence and the cross in his speeches and publications undergirded King's messages to blacks that there will be no freedom apart from suffering. The idea that the unearned suffering of blacks was redemptive appeared early in his theology and remained dominant throughout his life. When the bombing of his house aroused blacks to the potential for violence, King gave the anxious crowd in Montgomery a message that he would emphasize many times during his ministry:

We must not return violence under any condition. I know this is difficult advice to follow, especially since we have been the victims of
no less than ten bombings. But this is the way of Christ; it is the way
of the cross. We must somehow believe that unearned suffering is
redemptive.[10]

A similar emphasis on the necessity for suffering is found in Gandhi. Explicating *satyagraha* (soul force), Gandhi wrote: "[It] is the vindication of
truth not by infliction of suffering on the opponent but on one's self. . . .
Rivers of blood may have to flow before we gain our freedom, but it must
be our blood."

After much reflection on Gandhi's philosophy, and following a journey
to India during which he discussed his views with many scholars there,
King began to speak more forthrightly regarding the inevitability of black
suffering through nonviolence before the goal of an integrated, beloved
community can be achieved. No statement expressed this idea more forcefully than his often repeated statement:

We will match your capacity to inflict suffering with our capacity to
endure suffering. We will meet your physical force with soul force. We
will not hate you, but we cannot in all good conscience obey your unjust laws. Do to us what you will and we will still love you. Bomb our
homes and threaten our children; send your hooded perpetrators of
violence into our communities and drag us out on some wayside road,
beating us and leaving us half dead, and we will still love you. But we
will soon wear you down by our capacity to suffer. And in winning our
freedom we will so appeal to your heart and conscience that we will
win you in the process.[11]

There is no doubt that King was deeply influenced by Gandhi's philosophy of nonviolence as a potent weapon for the practical implementation of
Jesus' idea of love in the context of the black struggle for justice. But it is
obvious that his unshakeable commitment to nonviolence and the inevitability of black suffering was much more appealing to liberal whites than
to oppressed blacks. Many black scholars, like Kenneth Clark, warned
King of the psychological damage to black personality when black people
are urged to assume the heavy burden that his theology required.[12]

King's use of Thoreau's concept of civil disobedience was to come later in the course of his political development. Open disobedience to the law happened first during the sit-ins (1960), freedom rides (1961), and the Birmingham demonstrations (1963). Civil disobedience was initially limited to regional laws of discrimination against blacks in the South.

Thoreau said that "it is not desirable to cultivate a respect for the law, so much as for the right. The only obligation which I have the right to assume is to do at anytime what I think right."[13] A firm opponent of slavery, Thoreau was also jailed for his refusal to pay taxes to support the war with Mexico. When his friend Ralph Waldo Emerson reportedly asked, "Thoreau, why are you in jail?" Thoreau replied, "Emerson, why are you out of jail?"

Although Martin King could apply Thoreau's logic of civil disobedience in his protest against regional segregation laws of the South, he had more difficulty applying it to federal laws, because he used the federal laws as the basis for his disobedience of discriminatory laws of the South. He expected and received the legal support of the federal courts, the President, and the Congress in the achievement of black people's civil rights. His concern about federal support probably accounted for his retreat in the second attempt to cross the Pettus Bridge during the Selma to Montgomery march. In Memphis, however, he resolved to disobey a federal injunction against the march but was assassinated before it actually happened.

The Faith of the Black Church

Without seeking to minimize the importance of the other three sources, they should be interpreted in the light of the faith of the Black Church which decisively influenced the development and final shape of King's theology. King's theology was defined by the themes of justice, love, and hope. The meaning of each, while influenced by the other sources, achieved their distinctiveness as King attempted to fulfill his vocation as a black preacher. He believed that the gospel demanded that he speak the truth and that he work toward its establishment in human relations.

Justice, love, and hope are central themes in the history of the black religious tradition. It was black people's concern for justice in the church and society that led them to organize independent churches during the late eighteenth and early nineteenth centuries. It was their concern for love in human relations that prevented their fight for justice from degenerating into an attitude of vengeance and violence. It was black people's focus on God's eschatological hope that enabled them to "keep on keeping on," fighting for the right with love in their hearts, even though the achievement of justice seemed bleak and doubtful.

Martin King deeply internalized the values of the black religious tradition in which he was born.

> I am many things to many people; Civil Rights leader, agitator, trouble-maker and orator, but in the quiet resources of my heart, I am fundamentally a clergyman, a Baptist preacher. This is my being and my heritage for I am also the son of a Baptist preacher, the grandson of a Baptist preacher, and the great-grandson of a Baptist preacher. The Church is my life and I have given my life to the Church.[14]

The distinctiveness of King's ideas of justice, love, and hope were developed in the context of his vocation as pastor of Dexter and Ebenezer Baptist Churches and as president of SCLC, an organization composed mainly of preachers. His theology, therefore, can be properly understood only from the vantage point of his belief that he had been set aside by God to be the leader of blacks, the people whom he believed God had chosen to "save the soul of America." His belief that black people were called by God to redeem America through their suffering love was derived from the black religious tradition.

The most appropriate way to decide what was primary for King's theology is to identify the source to which he turned in moments of crisis during his fight for justice. Where he turned when his back was up against the wall and when everything seemed hopeless will tell us far more about his theology than the papers he wrote in graduate school. Engulfed by the "midnight of despair," where did he receive the hope that "morning will come?"[15]

The evidence is clear: Whether we speak of the Montgomery bus boycott, the Birmingham demonstrations, the Selma March, Black Power, or Vietnam, King turned to the faith of the Black Church in moments of frustration and despair. His existential appropriation of black faith occurred a few weeks after the inauguration of the Montgomery bus boycott. He not only referred to this event in his writings but especially in many of his sermons in black churches.[16] One night, January 27, 1956, King received a nasty telephone call: "Nigger, we are tired of you and your mess now and if you aren't out of this town in three days, we're going blow your brains out and blow up your house." Though he had received many similar threats (about forty daily), for some reason that one stunned him, preventing him from going to sleep. He began to realize that his wife and newly born baby daughter could be taken from him or he from them at any moment. He got up out of bed and went to the kitchen to heat some coffee, "thinking," he said, "that coffee would give me a little relief."

In the midst of one of the most agonizing experiences of his life, he searched for a place that he could stand. "I started thinking about many things; I pulled back on the theology and philosophy that I had just studied in the universities trying to give philosophical and theological reasons for the existence and the reality of sin and evil, but the answer didn't quite come there." Unable to cope with his frustration and despair, King turned to the God of the black faith that he had been taught as a child:

> Something said to me, you can't call on daddy now; he's in Atlanta, a hundred-seventy-five miles away. . . . You've got to call on that something, on that person that your daddy used to tell you about, that power that can make a way out of no way. And I discovered then that religion had to become real to me and I had to know God for myself. And I bowed down over that cup of coffee. I never will forget it. Oh yes, I prayed a prayer. And I prayed out loud that night. I said, "Lord, I'm down here trying to do what's right. I think I'm right. I think the cause that we represent is right. But Lord, I must confess that I'm weak now, I'm faltering, I'm losing my courage, and I can't let the people see me like this because if they see me weak and losing my courage they will begin to get weak."

It was in the midst of this crisis of faith that King experienced the liberating presence of God as never before. He heard an inner voice saying: "Martin Luther, stand up for righteousness. Stand up for justice. Stand up for truth. And lo, I will be with you, even until the end of the world." After that liberating experience he said: "I was ready to face anything."[17] From that point onward, King never doubted God's presence in the struggle for justice, reassuring him that love and nonviolence, despite the odds, will triumph over hate and violence.

King's theology was defined by an eschatological hope, God's promise not to leave the little ones alone in struggle. In his sermons, he spoke often of "midnight," "darkness," and the "cross," usually referring to racism, poverty, and war. But in spite of the great difficulties he encountered in fighting these evils, King was certain that "we shall overcome," because "truth crushed to the earth will rise again."

> Sometimes I feel discouraged. And I don't mind telling you this morning that sometimes I feel discouraged. I felt discouraged in Chicago. As I moved through Mississippi and Georgia and Alabama I feel discouraged. Living everyday under the threat of death I feel discouraged sometimes. Living everyday under extensive criticism, even from Negroes, I feel discouraged sometimes. Yes, sometimes I feel discouraged and feel my work's in vain, but then the Holy Spirit revives my soul again. There is a balm in Gilead to make the wounded whole.

The Function and Interrelationship of the Sources

The black religious tradition always remained at the heart of King's thought and practice, even though he rarely articulated its importance in most of his writings and speeches. He seldom referred to the theological significance of the Black Church, because almost everything he published was intended primarily for a white audience who had doubts about the legality and morality of nonviolent direct action and civil disobedience. Many whites complained about the violence which civil rights demonstrations evoked, and they strongly urged King to "wait," "cool off," and "not to move too fast." Martin King's frequent appeals to Gandhi and a variety of Euro-American theologians and philosophers were intended to persuade the white public that he had sound philosophical and Christian reasons for his nonviolent demonstrations. He wanted to demonstrate that his claim that "segregation is a cancer in the body politic" as well as a "tragic evil which is utterly unchristian" was not simply the rhetoric of a black preacher but was derived from the most influential thinkers in the West.

On the other hand, when Martin King spoke to an audience in a black church, he may have referred to white theologians and philosophers, but they were secondary to his overall purpose. Blacks did not need to be persuaded that segregation was morally evil and contrary to democratic values and thus should be eliminated. They needed inspiration and courage to struggle against tremendous odds. It was black people's faith that "God can make a way out of no way" that King knew in his heart and articulated so well in his sermons.

Focusing primarily on the themes of justice, love, and hope as they are grounded in faith, King integrated the four sources into a coherent whole, with each theme emerging as dominant at different periods of his life as he sought to communicate his ideas to black and white audiences. Protestant liberalism and the philosophies of Gandhi and Thoreau were the sources that provided the intellectual structure that King used to interpret his ideas and actions regarding nonviolence and civil disobedience to the white community. They gave him a method of fighting for justice that was consistent with American democratic values and the theological and philosophical tradition of the West.

When King spoke to a black audience, his chief source was the Bible, as mediated through the Black Church tradition. It can be said that as long as King was confident that justice would be achieved in a reasonable amount of time and with the support of the federal government, white moderates of the South and North, labor, and the churches, he relied primarily on liberal Protestantism, Gandhi, and Thoreau to express his theology. The dominant theme was always love with justice and hope interpreted in its light. But when the problem of injustice seemed insurmountable and the white support for justice was not visibly present, King turned to the faith of the Black Church, with an emphasis on God's eschatological promise to "transform dark yesterdays into bright tomorrows," "the fatigue of despair into the buoyancy of hope."

The faith of the Black Church and the integrationist tradition in black history provided the political and religious sources for expressing King's views to the black community. Because white racists controlled the centers of sociopolitical power, many blacks were paralyzed by the fear of loss of property and life. They were uncertain of their courage to challenge the white power structure and of their spiritual strength to sustain themselves in that challenge.

Furthermore, some blacks were not sure that integration into white society was the most appropriate goal of the Civil Rights movement or whether nonviolence was the right method for achieving that goal. The black political tradition of Frederick Douglass and the NAACP provided the rationale that integration was the correct political goal and that nonviolent direct action was the only way to achieve it. But it was the faith of the Black Church that provided black people with the courage to fight against great odds, giving them the hope that the goal of justice would eventually be achieved.

Change and Continuity in King's Theology

The function and interrelationship of the sources are illuminated when seen in the context of an analysis of the continuity and change in King's theology. The character of King's theological development was shaped by two overall concerns: what he was fighting *against* and what he was fighting *for*. He began his public ministry by fighting against racism, and the events of the 1960s forced him to connect it with poverty and militarism. Though King's theology went through several developmental changes between 1955 and 1968, this aspect of his thought should be analyzed in relation to the continuity in his thinking. As the changes can best be illuminated in relation to what he was fighting against and the strategies he developed to overcome evil, so the continuity in King's theology can best be demonstrated when it is analyzed in relation to what he was fighting for. King's goal was not simply the elimination of racism, poverty, and war, but rather the establishment of an integrated community of persons of all races, working together toward the building of the kingdom that he called the "beloved community." Everything King did and said regarding the church and society was intended to create a new community in which love and justice defined the relationship between all people.

Martin King began his public career with an emphasis on the justice of God. He derived its meaning from the Hebrew prophets, as interpreted in the faith and history of the Black Church and liberal Protestant theology. He also used the American democratic tradition, especially as found in the Constitution and the Declaration of Independence. As blacks in Montgomery began the bus boycott, King based their actions on the theme of justice in the Christian faith, and love and hope were interpreted in its light. But shortly after the boycott began, white and black advisors, concerned about the development of a method of social change that would avoid violence, urged King to adopt Gandhi's method of nonviolent direct action and thereby place love at the center of his thought. During this period, love replaced justice as the dominant theme, and King derived its meaning from the life and teachings of Jesus and Gandhi. Also useful were the theologians and philosophers he studied in graduate school. With an emphasis on love strongly influenced by liberal Protestantism, justice was defined as the absence of segregation and the establishment of an integrated community, and hope became similar to the liberal optimism that King had studied in graduate school.

When King realized that the life-chances of the poor had not been affected by the gains of the Civil Rights movement, that the federal government was not nearly as committed to fighting the war on poverty as it was to fighting the war in Vietnam and that white moderates were not as concerned with the establishment of justice in the North as they had been in fighting legal segregation in the South, the idea of hope became the dominant theme in his theology. His reflections on hope were derived almost exclusively from biblical religion as mediated through the faith and history of the Black Church. Hope was carved out of the suffering and disappointments he experienced in fighting injustice in urban ghettos (especially Chicago), in dialoguing with Black Power advocates, and in taking his stand against the war in Vietnam. He placed love and justice in an eschatological context, with an emphasis on bearing witness to God's coming freedom by taking a stand for justice *now*, even though the odds against its establishment are great.

Between 1955 and 1968, Martin King moved from an optimistic integrationist to a temporary separatist;[18] from a social reformer to a militant nonviolent revolutionary;[19] from an intellectual dependence on classical Western philosophy to a call for the study of black philosophers;[20] from a naive belief that southern white moderates (especially ministers) would join him in the struggle for an integrated society to a deepening skepticism regarding whether even white northern liberal Christians, labor, and government officials had the moral sensitivity to understand the depth of the disadvantages that African-Americans must overcome in order to survive in a society that does not recognize their humanity;[21] from his inspiring "I Have a Dream" oration to his despairing assertion that "the dream I had in Washington back in 1963 has often turned into a nightmare";[22] from his silence about the Vietnam war to his well-known "Beyond Vietnam" speech at New York's Riverside Church (April 4, 1967), proclaiming that "America is the greatest purveyor of violence in the world today."[23]

To understand the character of King's theological development, it is important to note its three phases, with each being defined by an emphasis on justice, love, and hope. When he reluctantly became the leader of the

Montgomery bus boycott, he was not an advocate of nonviolent direct action or a follower of Mahatma Gandhi. Indeed, as white violence increasingly emerged as a threat to his life, King applied for a license to carry a gun in his car but was refused by the Montgomery police department. The guiding principle for his initial involvement in the bus boycott was the justice of God as defined by the prophets and Jesus Christ. Reflecting back on the preparation for his first major speech at Holt Street Baptist Church (December 5, 1955), King said that his chief question was: "How could I make a speech that would be militant enough to keep my people aroused to positive action and yet moderate enough to keep this fever within controllable and Christian bounds?"[24]

After referring to the "right to protest" as an inherent part of American democracy, and then connecting what happened to Rosa Parks with the "long history of abuses and insults that Negro citizens had experienced on the city buses," King creatively articulated the balance between active protest and appropriate moderation with the passion and rhythm so typical of the best in the Black Church tradition. As he increased the volume of his voice, seeking to allow himself to be used by God's Spirit to empower poor blacks to "walk the streets in dignity rather than ride the bus in humiliation," King said:

> There comes a time when people get tired of being trampled over by the iron feet of oppression. There comes a time . . . when people get tired of being flung across the abyss of humiliation where they experience the bleakness of nagging despair. There comes a time when people get tired of being pushed out of the glittering sunlight of life's July and left standing amidst the piercing chill of an Alpine November. We are here this evening because we're tired now.[25]

Martin King justified the boycott on both legal and moral grounds, emphasizing that the "great glory of American democracy is the right to protest for right" and that the Christian faith demanded that black people "stand up for their rights." In sharp contrast to King's later description of this speech in *Stride Toward Freedom* in which he said "love your enemies" was his chief emphasis,[26] my examination of the tape and printed text revealed that *justice*, and not love was his major theme.

> We only assemble here because of our desire to see right exist. . . .
> We're going to work with grim and firm determination to gain justice

on the buses of this city. And we are not wrong . . . in what we are doing. If we are wrong, then the Supreme Court of this nation is wrong.
If we are wrong, the Constitution of the United States is wrong. If we
are wrong, God Almighty is wrong. If we are wrong, Jesus of Nazareth
was merely a utopian dreamer and never came down to earth. If we
are wrong, justice is a lie. . . . We are determined . . . to work and fight
until "justice runs down like waters and righteousness like a mighty
stream."[27]

There is a great difference between King's report of this speech in *Stride
Toward Freedom* and the tape of what he actually said on that occasion.
Even as King urged blacks to keep "God in the forefront," his emphasis re-
mained on justice and not love, coercion and not persuasion.

I want to tell you this evening that it is not enough for us to talk about
love. Love is one of the pinnacle parts of the Christian faith. There is
another side called justice. And justice is really love in calculation.
Justice is love correcting that which would work against love. The Almighty God . . . is not . . . just standing out saying, "Behold Thee, I
love you Negro." He's also the God that standeth before the nations
and says: "Be still and know that I am God, and if you don't obey me
I'm gonna break the backbone of your power, and cast you out of the
arms of your international and national relationships." Standing be-
side love is always justice. And we are only using the tools of justice.
Not only are we using the tools of persuasion but we've got to use the
tools of coercion.[28]

On the tape of King's Holt Street Address, there is no mention of Gandhi's method of nonviolent direct action and no reference to Jesus' command to "love your enemies." His stress was almost exclusively on justice
as defined by the American democratic tradition of equality and the biblical theme of the righteousness of God.

As King's involvement in the Montgomery bus boycott deepened and
the appeal for white support was accentuated, the Christian idea of love
emerged as the central theme of his theology. Love became the modifier of
justice as he sought to eradicate the fears of both blacks and whites regarding violence. By the time King wrote *Stride Toward Freedom* (1958), he had
become an international figure, with white and black advisors assisting
him in his work, including the editing of his book manuscript and ad-

dresses. I am convinced that the change in emphasis from justice to love was partly due to the editorial hand of his advisors.[29]

As the boycott proceeded, King's practical concern about the dangers of violence, along with his acceptance of the naive optimism of liberal theology, caused him to change his primary emphasis from justice to love. While acknowledging the important role of the Black Church and the absence of any reference to Gandhi, King seemed to have forgotten about his original accent on justice. For example, in *Stride Toward Freedom*, he recalls:

> The first days of the protest . . . the phrase most often heard was "Christian love." It was the Sermon on the Mount, rather than a doctrine of passive resistance, that initially inspired the Negroes of Montgomery to dignified social action. It was Jesus of Nazareth that stirred the Negroes to protest with the creative weapon of love.[30]

Likewise, King's focus on Gandhi and nonviolent resistance was a later development, emerging simultaneously with his new emphasis on love. The connection between Gandhi and the Montgomery bus boycott was suggested initially by Juliette Morgan's letter to the editor of the *Montgomery Advertiser*. Later on, nonviolent direct action was intellectually defined and practically implemented when Bayard Rustin and Glen E. Smiley of the Fellowship of Reconciliation (FOR) joined Martin King as advisors about two months after the boycott began.[31]

During the phase in which love was dominant in King's theology, he defined racism as segregation and designated it as America's "chief moral dilemma." But the more he fought racism the more he came to realize that it was much more complex than the discrimination laws in the South. To King's surprise, he not only found racism in the North, but discovered also that northern racism, though less visible, was more destructive to human personality and also more deeply embedded in the sociopolitical structures than what he had seen in the South.

After the Selma March and the passage of the Voting Rights Act (1965), several events caused King to undertake a deeper analysis of racism, which in turn disclosed the severe limitations of what had been achieved in the southern-based Civil Rights movement. Five days following the signing of the Voting Rights Bill by President Johnson (August 6), the Watts riot erupted (August 11), initiating a radical change in King's per-

spective regarding the nature of racism and what would be needed to eliminate it. His struggle and frustrations in Chicago, the rise of Black Power,
drastic cuts in the domestic budget, and a rapid escalation of expenditures
for the war in Vietnam—all these events contributed to King's movement
toward the left. His analysis of racism disclosed its global manifestations,
especially its connection with two other evils: poverty and war. King began to acknowledge publicly the limitations of his earlier views and started
to connect racism with "class issues . . . the privileged as over against the
underprivileged," and even openly advocating democratic socialism.[32]

When King saw the depth of the problem of racism as reflected by exten-
sive poverty in the northern ghettos and its devastating effects on the self-
worth of black people, he became so incensed that he could no longer keep
silent regarding the moral contradictions involved. It was during the period between the end of 1965 and his assassination in 1968 that Martin
King entered a revolutionary path that led him to declare "God's judgment
. . . on America" because of its failure to use its vast economic resources
for life rather than death.

> There is something wrong with our nation. Something desperately
> wrong. . . . There is confusion in the land. . . . This is why we've made
> a decision to come to the seat of government [and] will seek to say to
> the nation that if you don't straighten up, and that if you do not begin
> to use your vast resources of wealth to lift God's children from the
> dungeons of despair and poverty, then you are writing your own obit-
> uary. We are coming to Washington to say to America, "straighten
> up, and fly right."[33]

The primary source for King's prophetic critique of President Johnson's
war policies was the black church tradition. There is nothing in liberal
Protestant theology, Gandhi or Thoreau, or even the integrationist tradition of Douglass and the civil rights organizations that can explain the
content and the style of King's devastating critique of America's involvement in Vietnam. He was unrelenting in his criticisms, and he refused the
advice of any of his black and white friends who warned him about his lack
of competence in foreign policy and the danger of mixing peace and civil
rights. Some even questioned his patriotism. But King was quick to respond that he was speaking out against the war not because he was a civil
rights activist or an expert in foreign policy. He spoke solely in the name of

God's righteousness and human decency. As a minister of the God of Jesus, he could not keep silent, for the truth of the gospel was at stake.

Although his "Beyond Vietnam" address was perhaps his greatest hour and best known indictment of U.S. policies in Vietnam, it is in his unpublished sermons that one can clearly observe the depth of the agony of King's concerns and the source of his theological criticism. Most of these sermons were delivered at Ebenezer Baptist Church in Atlanta. Hardly anyone can read them or listen to the tapes and fail to acknowledge the decisive impact of the black and biblical traditions upon the content of his sermons and the forcefulness in which he delivered them. They include: "Why I Am Opposed to the War in Vietnam," "Mastering Our Fears," "The Drum Major Instinct," "A Knock at Midnight," "Standing by the Best in an Evil Time," "Who Is My Neighbor?," "Unfulfilled Dreams," and "But If Not. . . ."

In these sermons, King takes his stand with the prophets of the biblical tradition and rejects the advice of many of his friends and followers in SCLC, NAACP, labor, government, and even black and white churches, all of whom told him to keep silent about the war in Vietnam, because he was alienating President Johnson and the financial supporters of SCLC. With prophetic passion, so typical of the best in the Black Church tradition, King told them:

> I'm sorry, you don't know me. I'm not a consensus leader. I don't determine what is right and wrong by looking at the budget of the Southern Christian Leadership Conference, or by taking a Gallup Poll of the majority opinion. Ultimately a genuine leader is not a searcher for consensus but a molder of consensus.[34]

King deeply believed that just as Shadrach, Meshach, and Abednego had to take their stand against King Nebuchadnezzar and refuse to worship the King's golden image, even though they faced the flames of the fiery furnace, so he, Martin King, had to take his stand against Lyndon Johnson's war policies and refuse to bow down to the economic and political pressures of the State Department and its supporters. As the intensity of the pressures increased, even to the extent that the FBI was trying to force him to commit suicide, King turned to the God of black faith, because he believed that, as was true of the "three Hebrew children," God could deliver him "if it be so" (Dan. 3:17).

Using the response of the three Hebrews to Nebuchadnezzar as a sermon title, "But If Not . . . ,"[35] King made it clear that he was prepared to give his life for the truth of God. Nothing, absolutely nothing, was more important to Martin King than speaking and doing the truth. The more he was pressured to keep silent, the more forcefully he spoke out against the evils of racism, poverty, and war. In fact King became so disturbed about injustice that many of his biographers and some close friends have suggested that he was on the verge of a mental breakdown. I am sure that many contemporaries of the Hebrew prophets had similar feelings about them. The nature of the prophets' vocation almost always threw them into conflict with the values of their time. Prophets of every age are truthtellers, and the "powers that be" never want to hear the truth in a world based on their lies. When Whitney Young of the Urban League, a colleague and friend, cornered King in public and reprimanded him about his views on Vietnam, King responded sharply: "Whitney, what you are saying may get you a foundation grant but it will not get you into the kingdom of truth."

One cannot understand correctly Martin King's convictions about Vietnam, Black Power, racism, and poverty without a keen knowledge of the role of the "preacher as prophet" in the black community. When the black preacher is true to his/her vocational calling, he/she must speak the truth of God regardless of who is affected by its judgment. That was why King's most severe indictments against the evils of racism, poverty, and war were delivered as sermons. As a prophet of God, he had no choice but to speak the Word of God. In the sermon entitled "Standing by the Best in an Evil Time," King made a forceful and prophetic statement on why he could not keep silent on the evil of America's involvement in Vietnam.

> I've decided what I'm going to do. I ain't going to kill nobody in Mississippi [and] in Vietnam. I ain't going to study war no more. And you know what? I don't care who doesn't like what I say about it. I don't care who criticizes me in an editorial. I don't care what white person or Negro criticizes me. I'm going to stick with the best. On some positions, cowardice asks the question "is it safe?" Expediency asks the question, "is it politic?" Vanity asks the question, "is it popular?" But conscience asks the question, "is it right?" And there comes a time when a true follower of Jesus Christ must take a stand that's neither

safe nor politic nor popular but he must take that stand because it is right. Every now and then we sing about it, "if you are right, God will fight your battle." I'm going to stick by the best during these evil times.[36]

Conclusion

When Americans celebrate Martin Luther King, Jr.'s birthday as a national holiday, seminary students and faculty, church leaders and Christians throughout the world should not forget his importance *as theologian*, perhaps the most important in American history. In saying this, I do not wish to minimize the significant contribution of other theologians —whether Jonathan Edwards, Walter Rauschenbusch, or the Niebuhr brothers. There are three reasons that make Martin King a candidate for the status of America's most outstanding theologian:

1. If theology is a disciplined endeavor to interpret the meaning of the gospel for the present time, and if the gospel is God's liberation of the poor from bondage, then I would claim that no one has articulated the Christian message of freedom more effectively, prophetically, and creatively in America than Martin Luther King, Jr.

2. Unlike many American theologians who often look toward Europe to identify theological problems that require disciplined reflection, Martin King's theological perspective achieved its creativity by engaging uniquely American issues. He was truly an *American* theologian and not simply a theologian who happened to live in the United States. No theologian has made a greater impact on American culture than Martin Luther King, Jr. Making his birthday a national holiday merely symbolized that fact.

3. Unlike most white theologians who do theology as if their definitions of it are the only ones and as if their problems are the only ones that deserve the attention of disciplined theological reflection, Martin King did not limit his theological reflections to the problems of one group. While he began with a focus on the racial oppression of blacks, his theological vision was universal. He was as concerned about the liberation of whites from their oppression as oppressors as he was in eliminating the racial oppression of blacks. He was as concerned about the life-chances of brown children in Vietnam as he was about black children in America's cities. King's vision was truly international, embracing all humanity. That is why his

name is invoked by the oppressed around the world who are fighting for freedom. Teachers of theology do themselves, their students, and their discipline a great disservice when they ignore the outstanding contribution that King has made to American theology and to all who are seeking to understand the gospel today. For if one wishes to know what it means to be a theologian, there is no better example than Martin Luther King, Jr.

Martin Luther King, Jr.,
Black Theology—Black Church

D uring a decade of writing and teaching Black Theology, the most frequent question that has been addressed to me, publicly and privately,
by blacks and especially by whites, has been: "How do you reconcile the
separatist and violent orientation of black theology with Martin Luther
King's emphasis on integration, love, and nonviolence?" I have always
found it difficult to respond to this question because those who ask it seem
unaware of the interrelations between King, black theology, and the
Black Church.

While it is not my primary intention to compare King and black theology, I do hope that an explication of his theology in the context of the Black
Church will show, for those interested in a comparison, that black theology and King are not nearly as far apart as some persons might be inclined
to think.

I

The white public and also many white scholars have misunderstood King,
because they know so little about the Black Church community, ignoring
its effect upon his life and thought. An example of this misguided interpretation are the books by Kenneth Smith and Ira Zepp, Jr., *Search for the Beloved Community: The Thinking of Martin Luther King, Jr.* (Judson, 1974),
and John Ansbro, *The Mind of Martin Luther King, Jr.* (Orbis, 1982). These
authors analyze the thought of Martin King as if the Black Church community had no decisive impact on him, indeed as if thought itself is limited
to the white intellectual community. While these books are useful in telling us what King learned in graduate school and what intellectual re-

sources he used in communicating his ideas to the white community, they are not helpful in identifying the heart of King's theology and faith that sustained him in his fight for justice.

When one uses exclusively the perspectives of white theologians to interpret Martin King, it is difficult to explain the consistency of his thinking and actions. How is it possible for King to reconcile his use of the neo-orthodox theology of Reinhold Niebuhr and the Boston Personalism of Edgar S. Brightman? King appeals to so many resources for his ideas that it is conceptually impossible to reconcile them into one coherent whole when these white philosophers and theologians are used as the primary source of their origin and analysis. That is why many of King's interpreters find it nearly impossible to explain the entirety of his theological perspective in a consistent and wholistic manner.

What is true for the interpreters of Martin King is also true for many interpreters of my own perspective on black theology. As King used evangelical liberalism and Boston Personalism in defining his theology, many of my interpreters claim that I use the so-called neo-orthodox theology of Karl Barth. When I also begin to use Tillich, Marx, Bonhoeffer, and other white interpreters for the presentation of my ideas, my interpreters get a little confused in explicating the consistency of my perspective, because the different ideas I use for interpreting black theology do not belong in the same theological school of thought.

What is most interesting is that even I myself used to think that the sources for explaining my theology were Barth, Bonhoeffer, and Tillich, because these were the theologians who made the most conscious intellectual impact on me during my seminary days. After writing a Ph.D. dissertation on Karl Barth's anthropology, I naturally turned to him for communicating my deepest feelings about the theological implications of the black struggle for freedom. At that time, Barth and others like him were the only intellectual resources at my command for explicating the theological meaning of the black struggle, even though the truth of it did not arise from the experience of white neo-orthodox theologians.

Since the publication of *Black Theology and Black Power* (1969), I have come to realize the limitation of this procedure and have attempted to correct it as much as possible, while not denying the usefulness of ideas from all cultures. I now know that even though I may not have recognized it, the Black Church was and still is the most dominant element for a proper understanding of my own theological perspective. While I do not rule out other influences, they are not in any way decisive. I can discard Barth and Tillich as easily as I can choose to use them. They, as well as others, are merely instrumental in giving conceptual structure to a primary commitment determined by the Black Church community.

II

With that community in mind, one can then understand both the similarities and differences between King's theology and my own perspective on black theology. Although our differences on violence versus nonviolence, love and reconciliation, and the possibility of change in the white community are real, they are differences between two persons who are deeply committed to the same faith of the Black Church. Our differences are not so great as is usually believed. They are more semantic than substantive, and can best be understood by investigating our different circumstances in the black community and the audiences to which we address our viewpoints.

King was not nearly as nonviolent as many claimed, and his faith in whites and the accomplishment of his movement was not uncritical. For example, when he spoke about black progress in the area of civil rights, he knew that all was not as well as whites liked to think and that for the masses of blacks the movement had left their situation of oppression untouched. In a 1965 interview with Alex Haley, King said:

> Though many would prefer not to, we must face the fact that progress for the Negro—to which white moderators like to point in justifying gradualism—has been relatively insignificant, particularly in terms of the Negro masses. What little progress has been made—and that includes the Civil Rights Act—has applied primarily to the middle class Negro. Among the masses, especially in the Northern ghettoes, the situation remains the same, and for some it is worse.[1]

Speaking about his disappointment regarding southern white ministers, King said:

> The most pervasive mistake I have made was in believing that because our cause was just, we could be sure that the white ministers of the South, once their Christian consciences were challenged, would rise to our aid. . . . I ended up, of course, chastened and disillusioned.[2]

Both of these quotations show that Martin King did face the failure of the Civil Rights movement to reach the masses of black people. He also realized that whites, even liberal clergy, could not always be counted on to act out in life what they claim in their confessions of faith or in their theological textbooks.

My own perspective on black theology, unlike Martin King, begins with the assumption that the people who benefit from the unjust social, political, and economic order are not likely to be the ones who will change it radically. I do not make this claim because I think that whites are by na- — *Malcolm* ture more evil than any other group of people. I make this claim because of the Christian doctrine of sin which says that individuals or groups will claim more than what they ought to, if they can get away with it. I think that the reality of sin has already been validated by history. I do not believe that any group of people will do right, because of the demands of faith *True* alone.

As Reinhold Niebuhr forcefully demonstrated in his *Moral Man and Immoral Society,* individuals may stand outside of themselves and therefore act against their interests as defined by the existing social arrangements. But groups seldom, if ever, can transcend their interests for the sake of another. Martin King was certainly aware of Niebuhr's analysis, but it apparently made little impact on his theological consciousness, since his optimism regarding whites could not be shaken radically. King's optimism, however, is not derived primarily from the theological liberalism of Boston Personalism or of the Social Gospel movement.

I think King received this faith in whites from the Black Church tradition which has always extended its openness to reconciliation to the white community. What is most amazing about the black community as a whole and the Black Church in particular is their willingness to forgive whites their brutality during slavery, lynching, and even oppression today in the ghettos of the urban cities. But despite our willingness to extend the right hand of fellowship, whites continue their massive assault upon the humanity of our people and get angry with us if we say we don't like it. It seems that whites have been allowed to do what they wish to us so long that they regard such inhumane invasion of black humanity as synonymous with their freedom.

With regard to what black people can expect from white people in our struggle for freedom, there are some genuine differences between King and me. I do not believe that whites or any other group holding power will voluntarily empower those who are powerless. Freedom is not a gift but must be taken. While the Gospel of God can and does empower people to change sides in the struggle for freedom, we must realize that many people publicly testify that they are for the poor but are in fact against them.

Even though there are important differences between King and me, I think they can best be understood from within the context of the Black Church rather than in the context of white liberal and neo-orthodox theologies of North America and Europe. Such views as represented by King and me, as well as many others, can be found throughout the black religious tradition. There is no need to turn to white Western theology for an explanation. King's perspective has its antecedents in Frederick Douglass, while my view is partly found in the life and writings of Henry Highland Garnet, both of whom were contemporaries in the nineteenth century and stressed somewhat different views regarding the place of whites in the black struggle for freedom.[3]

III

What was the main content of King's thought which he derived from the Black Church tradition? This question is not easy to answer because the Black Church has not done much systematic reflection in the area of theology. Our theologies have been presented in the forms of sermons, songs, prayers, testimonies, and stories of slavery and oppression. In these sources we have given our views of God and the world, and how each may be understood in relation to our struggle for freedom. We did not write essays on Christian doctrine because our descendents came as slaves from Africa and not as free people from Europe. Many blacks were prevented from learning to read and write either by the circumstances of our birth or by the legal restrictions defined by the government. Therefore, we had to do theology in forms other than rational reflections. We sang and preached our theology in worship and other sacred contexts. The central meaning disclosed in these nonrational sources is found in both their *form* and *content* and is identical with *freedom* and *hope*.

The influence of the Black Church and its central theme of freedom and hope can be seen in the language of King's speaking and writing. Everything he said and wrote sounds like a black sermon and not rational reflection. To be sure, King finished first in his class at Crozer and also wrote a Ph.D. dissertation at Boston on Henry Nelson Wieman's and Paul Til-lich's conceptions of God. But it is significant to note that he did not adopt the style of theological presentation from any of his white theological men-tors. He may have referred to white theologians and philosophers when he needed to explain his views to a white public, but the style of his presenta-tion was unmistakably from the tradition of black preaching.

Like his predecessors and contemporaries in the Black Church, King preached his theology, because the theme of freedom and hope had to be reflected in the movement and rhythm of his voice, if he expected a black congregation to take his message seriously. The eschatological hope of freedom is not only an idea to be analyzed in the conceptual language of white theologians and philosophers. It is primarily an event to be experi-enced when God's word of freedom breaks into the lives of the gathered community through the vehicle of the sermon's oration. No one under-stood the relationship between style and meaning in the context of the Black Church any better than Martin King.

In the Black Church, the meaning is found not primarily in the intellec-tual content of the spoken word but in the *way* the word is spoken and its effect upon those who hear it. That was why King could speak on Plato, Augustine, or even Boston Personalism, about which most blacks know nothing and care even less, and still move the congregation to tears and shouts of praise, even though they did not understand the content of his discourse. What they understood was the appropriate tone and movement of his speech which the people believe is the instrument for the coming presence of God's Spirit, thereby empowering them with the hope for free-dom. The people believe that freedom is coming because a foretaste of it is given in the sermon event itself. When King spoke of his dream at the 1963 March on Washington, and when he spoke the night before his assassina-tion in Memphis of his hope that we will reach the Promised Land, black people did not believe him because of the cogency of his logic but rather because of the spirit of empowerment generated by the style of his sermon oration. The people believed him because they contended that they experi-enced in their hearts the Spirit of God's liberating presence.

I think style is important in doing theology, and I try to reflect it in my own theology. How can black theology claim to be derived from the black community if it does not reflect in its style the language of the people? If black people do not recognize themselves in the language of theology, how can theology really claim blackness as its identity? For any theology to be truly black, its blackness must be expressed in the form in which it is written. This point was impressed on my own theological consciousness by the black critics of my early books *Black Theology and Black Power* (1969) and *A Black Theology of Liberation* (1970). With the publication of *The Spirituals and the Blues* (1972), *God of the Oppressed* (1975), *My Soul Looks Back* (1982), and other subsequent writings, I have tried to incorporate the *content* of liberation not only in theology but also in the very form of the language itself. Martin King has been helpful in the accomplishment of this task.

IV

In addition to the style of King's theology pointing toward freedom and hope, the same theme is also found in the *content* of his message. The influence of the Black Church on the content of King's theology is not easy to demonstrate. Anyone can easily notice the influence of the Black Church on his sermonic delivery and in the form of his writings. But that is not the case with the content of his message, since he does not explicitly refer to the Black Church. What is clear, however, is that the central theme of freedom and hope do define the content of King's life and message. It is summarized in his March on Washington speech:

> I have a dream that my four little children will one day live in a nation where they will not be judged by the color of their skin but by the content of their character. . . . With this faith we will be able to transform the jangling discords of our nation into a beautiful symphony of brotherhood. With this faith we will be able to work together, to pray together, to struggle together, to go to jail together, to stand up for freedom together, knowing that we will be free one day.

The words were spoken in 1963, but few of us today can speak with the confidence of Martin King, because events since that time are difficult to reconcile with his optimism. Between 1965 and 1968, even King had to move away from the optimism defined in the 1963 Washington speech, because his sermons and speeches did not dislodge the entrenchment of white power as he appeared to think. But despite the failure of his sermons and speeches to move whites to change the social, political, and economic situation, the content of his message of freedom and hope did move blacks to action. Without the response of the Black Church people, King would have had his hope for freedom destroyed, because even liberal whites seemed incapable of embodying the hope and freedom about which he preached.

In the Black Church, King knew that the people had a hope that stretched back to the beginnings of the black Christian community in the eighteenth and nineteenth centuries. All he had to do was restate that hope for freedom in the songs and language of the people and they would respond to the content of the message. That was why King used the language of the so-called Negro Spirituals in his sermons in black churches. His sermons always contained the hope for freedom, and he always related it to his current struggles to attain freedom in this world. But when it seemed as if freedom was difficult to realize in this world, Martin King did not despair but moved its meaning to an eschatological realm as defined by the Black Church's claim that "the Lord will make a way somehow." The night before he was assassinated, King, in a Black Church worship service, restated that hope with the passion and certainty so typical of the black preacher: "I may not get there with you, but I want you to know tonight that we as a people will get to the Promised Land. . . . Mine eyes have seen the glory of the coming of the Lord."

King's emphasis on the eschatological hope of freedom as defined by "the coming of the Lord" was not derived from white theologians and philosophers, but from his own religious tradition. These words of faith and hope were derived from the black tradition as defined by our pain and suffering. People who have not lived in the context of hundreds of years of slavery and suffering are not likely to express an eschatological hope of freedom. Hope in God's coming eschatological freedom is always derived from the suffering of people who are seeking to establish freedom on earth but have failed to achieve it. In their failure to establish freedom in their existing present, black people prevented despair from becoming the defining characteristic of their lives by looking forward to God's coming, eschatological freedom.

As with King, black theology, and the Black Church generally, we blacks do not deny that trouble is present in black life. What we deny is that it has the last word, for we believe, in the words of Charles Tindley, that "we will understand it better by and by."

Trials dark on every hand, and we cannot understand.
All the ways that God would lead us to the Blessed
    Promised Land
But he guides us with his eye and we'll follow till
    we die.
For we'll understand it better by and by.

By and by, when the morning comes,
All the saints of God are gathered home
We'll tell the story how we've overcome
For we'll understand it better by and by.

Martin Luther King, Jr.,
and the Third World

When Martin Luther King, Jr., achieved international fame as the leader of the Montgomery bus boycott in 1955–56, no African country below the Sahara had achieved political independence from the colonial regimes of Europe. When he was assassinated in Memphis, Tennessee, twelve years later, in 1968, the great majority of African countries had gained their independence. Since 1968 black Africans have continued their "stride toward freedom," overcoming the political domination of Europeans in every country except South Africa.[1]

As in Africa, similar struggles for freedom occurred in Asia and Latin America. The struggles of the poor in all societies remind us that the fires of freedom are burning and that nothing short of justice for all will establish peace and tranquility in the world.

As we reflect on the significance of the life and thought of Martin Luther King, Jr., for the people of America, it is important to remember that the meaning of his life is not bound by race, nationality, or creed. Speaking of the international significance of his son, Daddy King was correct when he said: "He did not belong to us, he belonged to the world."[2] I would add that Martin Luther King, Jr., belonged particularly to the Third World, the world of the poor and the disinherited. It is therefore important to ask about his significance for peoples of Africa, Asia, and Latin America and about their significance for him. In this essay I will limit my analysis to the impact of Third World liberation movements on the development of King's theology.

Martin King's thinking falls into two periods.[3] The first began with the Montgomery bus boycott in December 1955 and ended with the enactment of the Voting Rights Act in August 1965. The second period commenced in the fall of 1965 as King began to analyze more deeply the interrelationship of racism, poverty, and militarism in the policies of the United States government. In both periods his ideas were defined by his faith in the God of justice, love, and hope. The difference between the two periods is the shifting emphases he gave to each of those theological attributes as he sought to develop a nonviolent philosophy of social change that would eliminate racial and economic exploitation and establish peace in America and the world.

During the first period, King's thinking was defined by an optimistic belief that justice could be achieved through love, which he identified with nonviolence. The place of the Third World liberation movements in his thinking was to reinforce his liberal optimism regarding the certainty of the rise of a new world order of freedom and equality. In the early months of the Montgomery bus boycott, Martin King began to interpret the black struggle for justice in America as "a part of [an] overall movement in the world in which oppressed people are revolting against . . . imperialism and colonialism." He believed that black people's fight against segregation in America expressed the same spirit that led Africans, Asians, and Latin Americans to revolt against their European colonizers. Both revolts (that of blacks in America and that of the poor in the Third World), according to King, signified "the birth of a new age." Using that phrase for the title of an address in 1956, he said that Third World people had "lived for years and centuries under the yoke of foreign power, and [that] they were dominated politically, exploited economically, segregated and humiliated."[4] Because King saw little difference between colonialism in Africa and segregation in America, he employed the same language to describe both experiences. Speaking about the impatience of black and Third World peoples with oppression, King repeated the words he had first used at the Holt Street Baptist Church in 1955:

> There comes a time when people grow tired, when the throbbing desires of freedom begin to break forth. There comes a time when people get tired of being trampled over by the iron feet of the tramper. There comes a time when people get tired of being plunged across the abyss of exploitation, where they have experienced the bleakness and madness of despair. There comes a time when people get tired of being pushed out of the glittering sunlight of life's July and left standing in the pitying state of an Alpine November.[5]

In this and many similar statements, King's point was to emphasize that black and Third World people were fed up with segregation and colonialism. "In the midst of their tiredness," something happened to them. They began to reevaluate themselves, and as a result, they "decided to rise up in protest against injustice." The protests of the oppressed throughout the world, King believed, were nothing but a signal that "the time for freedom has come." No resistance from the oppressors could abort freedom's birth because, as King often said (quoting Victor Hugo), "there is no greater power on earth than an idea whose time has come."[6] Martin King's travel to the independence celebration of Ghana (1957), the rapid achievement of independence by other Third World nations, and his study tour of India (1959) deepened his optimism that freedom would soon be achieved.[7]

King's optimism regarding the prospect of freedom's achievement was derived partly from the success of the Civil Rights movement in America and liberation movements in the Third World. The Montgomery bus boycott, sit-ins and freedom rides, the demonstrations in Birmingham, the March on Washington, the Selma March, and other less publicized civil rights victories throughout the South—all were linked with the success of anticolonialist movements in the Third World. King believed that freedom's time had come, because oppressed peoples all over the world were demonstrating that they would no longer accept passively their exclusion from the material riches of God's creation.

In Martin King's view, segregation in America and colonialism in the Third World were nothing but the denial of the dignity and worth of human beings. Both the segregationist and the colonialist said by their actions that blacks and other coloreds are inferior beings, incapable of governing themselves or living in a relationship of equality with white Americans and Europeans. As long as there was insufficient resistance from black and Third World peoples, the old order of segregation and colonialism remained unchanged. The new age of freedom began to break forth when a "New Negro" was born in America and a "New Human Being" began to rise up from among the ragged and hungry masses of the world. Armed with a new sense of dignity and self-respect, both started to march together toward the promised land of freedom.

Of course, Martin King was aware that oppressors do not voluntarily grant freedom to the oppressed. He was also aware that white segregationists and European colonists had much more military power than their victims. Yet he contended that the coming of a new world order of freedom was inevitable. How could he be so sure? The answer is found in his faith in the biblical God of justice, love, and hope. No idea or strategy that King advocated can be understood correctly apart from his deep faith in the Christian God as defined by the black Baptist and liberal Protestant traditions. The new age is coming and cannot be stopped, because God, who is just and loving, wills that the oppressed be liberated. That is why King could say:

> Oppressed people cannot remained oppressed forever. The urge for freedom will eventually come. This is what happened to the American Negro. Something within has reminded him of his birthright of freedom; something without has reminded him that he can gain it. Consciously and unconsciously, he has been swept in by what the Germans call the Zeitgeist, and with his black brothers of Africa, and his brown and yellow brothers of Asia, South America, and the Caribbean, he is moving with a sense of cosmic urgency toward the promised land of racial justice.[8]

King often employed the German word Zeitgeist to refer to his belief that "the universe is under the control of a loving purpose, and that in the struggle for righteousness [we have] cosmic companionship." That is what he had in mind when he said that Rosa Parks "had been tracked down by the Zeitgeist—the spirit of the times."[9]

The role of God in King's idea of the coming new age is reflected also in his use of the striking image of the "dream." He spoke often of the "American Dream," referring to the idea of equality in the Declaration of Independence, the Constitution, and the Jewish-Christian Scriptures. King's dream, however, was not limited to racial equality in the United States but was defined by its universality and eternality. To say that the dream is universal means that it is for all—blacks and whites, men and women, the peoples of Africa, Asia, and Latin America, and those of the United States and Europe. To say that it is eternal means that equality is not a right conferred by the state; it is derived from God, the creator of all life.[10]

When Martin King urged people to "make the dream a reality" or to "face the challenge of a new age," he almost always told them to "develop a world perspective." "All life is inter-related," because God is the creator of all. "No individual . . . [or] nation can live alone," because we are made for each other. No people can be who they ought to be until others are who they ought to be. "This is the way the world is made."[11]

When Martin King received the Nobel Peace Prize in 1964, it deepened his commitment to global justice and peace and reinforced his belief that God willed it. "I have the audacity to believe," he said in his acceptance speech, "that people everywhere can have three meals a day for their bodies, education and culture for their minds, and dignity, equality and freedom for their spirits." For King, the Nobel Prize was an "unutterable fulfillment," given in recognition of those fighting for freedom all over the world. His dream of a coming new age of freedom is eloquently expressed in his Nobel Lecture.

> What we are seeing now is a freedom explosion. . . . The deep rumbling of discontent that we hear today is the thunder of disinherited masses, rising from dungeons of oppression to the bright hills of freedom. . . . All over the world, like a fever, the freedom movement is spreading in the widest liberation in history. The great masses of people are determined to end the exploitation of their races and land. They are awake and moving toward their goal like a tidal wave. You can hear them rumbling in every village, street, on the docks, in the houses, among the students, in the churches and at political meetings.[12]

Because God is involved in the freedom struggles, King believed, they cannot be halted. Victory is inevitable. Success in the Civil Rights and Third World liberation movements combined with his deep faith in God's loving justice gave King an optimistic hope that freedom was not too far away.

Turning to the second period of King's thought, 1965–68, I want to emphasize that certain bedrock ideas did *not* change. He did not change his mind about the basic principles of his faith or about the Civil Rights movement's goal of freedom. In fact, his convictions regarding God's will to inaugurate a new age of freedom deepened in the last years as he gave himself totally to the struggles for justice and peace in America and the world. His faith in nonviolence remained completely unshakable. What then was new or newly emphasized in the later period?

One new thing was his great disappointment with the failure of the majority of white moderates in the North and South (in government, labor, church, business, and even the Civil Rights movement) to support the goal of genuine equality for blacks and poor people. For several years he thought that he could win the support of the decent "white majority" in America through a moral appeal to religion and the democratic traditions that they claimed to live by. But as early as his *Playboy* interview (January 1965), he acknowledged his great letdown regarding government officials and white moderates:

> [A]bysmal ignorance seems to prevail among many state, city, and even Federal officials on the whole question of racial justice and injustice. . . . But this white failure to comprehend the depth and dimension of the Negro problem is far from being peculiar to government officials. . . . It seems to be a malady even among those whites who like to regard themselves as "enlightened." . . . I wonder at [persons] who dare to feel that they have some paternalistic right to set the timetable for another [person's] liberation. Over the past several years, I must say, I have been gravely disappointed with such white "moderates." I am often inclined to think that they are more of a stumbling block to the Negro's progress than the White Citizen's Counciler or the Ku Klux Klanner.[13]

When summer riots became a regular occurrence during the second half of the 1960s, King grew impatient with whites who withdrew their support from the Civil Rights movement and began to say that "law and order" ought to be the highest priority of government. "I say to you," proclaimed King, "the riots are caused by nice gentle, timid white moderates who are more concerned about order than justice."[14]

Another new disappointment for Martin King was his failure to win the support of the majority of blacks to nonviolent direct action as the primary method for gaining their freedom. The Watts riot (August 1965) and others that followed in the urban centers (along with the Black Power movement) revealed the great gap between King's optimism about nonviolence and the despair expressed in the random violence of American ghettos.

During the first ten years, King and others in the southern-based Civil Rights movement had assumed that blacks in the North would benefit in a derivative fashion from the victories gained in the South. The Watts riot and the subsequent rise of Black Power during the Meredith March (June 1966) showed that King had badly miscalculated the self-esteem that northern blacks would receive from the "straightened up backs" of southern blacks. When he went to Watts, he was surprised that many blacks there had never heard of him and even more astonished when he heard a group of young blacks boasting, "We won." "How can you say you won," King asked, "when thirty-four Negroes are dead, your community is destroyed, and whites are using the riots as an excuse for inaction?" "We won because we made them pay attention to us," they responded to him.[15] When King reflected on that response and the hostile reactions his message of nonviolence received from Chicago street gangs and young Black Power advocates during the Meredith March, he began to realize that the Civil Rights Act (1964) and the Voting Rights Act (1965) did not significantly affect the problems of racism and poverty, especially among northern blacks.

Martin King experienced a third disappointment. He expected American blacks' success with nonviolence to help persuade the majority of the oppressed of Africa, Asia, and Latin America to adopt a similar method in their struggles for freedom. But instead of adopting the creative method of nonviolence, many Third World people were openly advocating armed revolution. King was aware that even some theologians in Latin America were joining revolutionary groups in their efforts to overthrow oppressive governments.

All of this caused him to reevaluate *not* the efficacy of nonviolence, but the depth of the problem of injustice in a global context. When King began seriously to analyze global injustice, he concluded that the three evils of racism, poverty, and militarism were interrelated and deeply rooted in both the sociopolitical life of America and the international economic order. King's focus on the global implications of racism in relation to poverty and war led him to conclude that the slums in American cities were a "system of internal colonialism" not unlike the exploitation of the Third World by European nations.[16]

King's global vision helped him to see that the sociopolitical freedom of blacks was closely tied to the liberation of their sisters and brothers in Africa, Asia, and Latin America. Token integration (that is, a few professionals moving into the existing mainstream of American society) was not true freedom. "Let us," wrote King in 1967, "not think of our movement as one that seeks to integrate the Negro into all the existing values of American society."[17]

The economic exploitation of Third World nations and the deepening poverty of the poor in the United States led King to the conclusion that there was something desperately wrong with America.

> Why are there forty million poor people in a nation overflowing with such unbelievable affluence? Why has our nation placed itself in the position of being God's military agent on earth, and intervened reck-lessly in Vietnam and the Dominican Republic? Why have we substi-tuted the arrogant undertaking of policing the whole world for the high task of putting our own house in order?

These questions suggested to King the "need for a radical restructuring of the architecture of American society," so that it can serve the needs of hu-manity throughout the world.[18]

The later years of Martin King's theology are also defined by a shift in the emphasis and meaning given the themes of love, justice, and hope. Ex-cept for his great Holt Street Address, with its powerful focus on justice, the first period of King's spiritual and intellectual development centered on love, with justice and hope being interpreted in its light. But as a result of the experiences and bleak reflections just described, hope becomes the center of Martin King's thinking, with love and justice being interpreted in *its* light. The main difference between his early and later years in regard to hope was this: In the early period, King's hope was similar to a naive op-timism, because it was partly based on the progress of the freedom move-ment in America and the Third World and the support it received both from the oppressed (by their active commitment to nonviolence) and from the majority in the dominant classes (by their apparent commitment to formal equality). In contrast, King's hope, in the later years, was not based on the backing he received from blacks and whites in the United States or from the international community. Rather, his hope was grounded almost exclusively on his faith in the God of the biblical and black traditions who told him, during the early months of the Montgomery bus boycott: "Stand up for righteousness. Stand up for justice. Stand up for truth. And lo I will be with you, even until the end of the world."[19]

Instead of trusting human allies to produce a victory over the forces of organized evil, King's hope was now a transcendent one, focusing on the biblical God of the oppressed who "put down the mighty from their thrones, and exalted those of low degree."[20] The shift came out in his critique of United States policy in Vietnam, which he knew would alienate his former allies.

Among the many disappointments that shaped the second period of his thinking, none pained King more than America's military involvement in Vietnam and the criticisms he received from his white and black friends (in government, the media, and the Civil Rights movement) for opposing it. The escalation of the war in Vietnam by the United States, along with a de-escalation of the War on Poverty, and American indifference toward massive poverty in the Third World motivated King to become one of the severest critics of the domestic and foreign policies of his government during the second half of the 1960s. He began to speak like a prophet, warning of the Day of Judgment, proclaiming God's wrath and indignation on a rich and powerful nation that was blind to justice at home and indifferent to world peace. Instead of speaking of the American dream as he had done so eloquently in the first half of the 1960s, he began to speak, over and over again, of an American nightmare, especially in Vietnam.[21]

Martin King did not enjoy criticizing his government. He loved America deeply, particularly its democratic and religious traditions of equality and justice. But he could not overlook the great contradictions of racism, poverty, and militarism. For King there was no greater inconsistency between creed and deed than America's military adventures in Vietnam. He frequently referred to Vietnam as a small nation whose own document of freedom, declaring independence from France in 1945, had quoted our Declaration of Independence. "Yet," King said, "our government refused to recognize them. President Truman said they were not ready for independence. So we fell victim as a nation at that time of the same deadly arrogance that has poisoned the international situation for all these years."[22]

The arrogance King referred to was racism. He believed "our disastrous experiments in Vietnam and the Dominican Republic have been . . . a result of racist decision making. Men of the white West . . . have grown up in a racist culture, and their thinking is colored by that fact. . . . They don't really respect anyone who is not white." King also felt that the vehement criticisms of his opposition to the Vietnam War emanating from the white community were motivated by racism. He spoke against his white allies in government and the media who had supported his stand on nonviolence during the sit-ins and freedom rides and in Birmingham and Selma and then rejected his position on Vietnam.

> They applauded us in the sit-in movement when we nonviolently de-
> cided to sit in at lunch counters. They applauded us on the freedom
> rides when we accepted blows without retaliation. They praised us in
> . . . Birmingham and Selma, Alabama. Oh, the press was so noble in
> its applause and . . . praise when I would say "Be nonviolent toward
> Bull Connor. . . . Be nonviolent toward Jim Clark." There is something
> strangely inconsistent about a nation and a press that would praise
> you when you say, "Be nonviolent toward Jim Clark," but will curse
> and damn you when you say, "Be nonviolent toward little brown Viet-
> namese children!"[23]

Martin King refused to accept the idea that being an American citizen obligated him to support his country in an unjust war. He refused to equate "dissent with disloyalty," as many of his critics did. On the contrary, he contended that he was the true patriot, because in his opposition to the war, he was in reality defending America's tradition of freedom and de-mocracy, which was being violated in Vietnam. Furthermore, King be-lieved that as a Nobel Laureate he was obligated to transcend nationalism, and thereby to take a stand for world peace. But much more important than his obligation as a citizen of the United States or of the world was his vocation as a minister of God. When people queried him about the wisdom of mixing peace and civil rights, King responded:

> Before I was a civil rights leader, I answered a call, and when God
> speaks, who can but prophesy? I answered a call which left the spirit
> of the Lord upon me and anointed me to preach the gospel. . . . I de-
> cided then that I was going to tell the truth as God revealed it to me.
> No matter how many people disagreed with me, I decided that I was
> going to tell the truth.[24]

For Martin King, telling the truth meant proclaiming God's judgment on America for its failure to use its technological resources for the good of humanity. "Here we spend thirty-five billion dollars a year to fight this ter-rible war in Vietnam and just the other day the Congress refused to vote forty-four million to get rid of rats in the slums and the ghettoes of our country." "The judgment of God is on America now," he said. He compared America to the rich man, Dives, who passed by the poor man, Lazarus, and never saw him. And like Dives, who went to hell because he refused to use his wealth to bridge the gulf that separated him from Lazarus, "America," King said, "is going to hell too, if she fails to bridge the gulf" that separates blacks from whites, the United States and Europe from the Third World.[25]

Because Martin King believed that America's war in Vietnam violated its own democratic values and the moral principles of the universe, he could not keep silent. There comes a time "when silence is betrayal." A nation that spends five hundred thousand dollars to kill an enemy soldier in Vietnam and only fifty dollars to get one of its citizens out of poverty is a nation that will be destroyed by its own moral contradictions. "If something doesn't happen soon," King said, "I'm convinced that the curtain of doom is coming down on the U.S."[26]

Although King was often depressed about his government's refusal to stop the war in Vietnam and to eliminate poverty at home and in the Third World, he did not lose hope. In December 1967, in "A Christmas Sermon on Peace," he proclaimed that despite the nightmare of racism, poverty, and war, "I still have a dream, because . . . you can't give up on life. If you lose hope . . . you lose that courage to be, that quality that helps you to go on in spite of all."[27]

It was Martin King's hope that sustained him in the midst of controversy, enabling him to make solidarity with the victims of the world, even though he failed to achieve the justice for which he gave his life. King's hope was grounded in the saving power of the cross of Jesus Christ, and it enabled him to see the certainty of victory in the context of an apparent defeat.

> When you stand up for justice, you never fail. The forces that have the power to make concession to the forces of justice and truth . . . but refuse to do it . . . are the forces that fail. . . . If there is no response from the federal government, from the Congress, that's the failure, not those who are struggling for justice.[28]

It is difficult for people who do not share Martin King's faith or his solidarity with the Third World to understand his meaning for poor people today. King's name is well known and greatly admired in the Third World because his life and thought disclose profound insights about humanity that are relevant to all who struggle for freedom.

"There is nothing in all the world greater than freedom."[29] Martin King gave his life for it. South African blacks, endowed with the same liberating spirit, are facing death daily, because they do not believe that whites have the right to determine the nature and the date of their freedom. Poor people throughout the world are demonstrating with their bodies that one cannot begin to live until one is ready to die for freedom.[30] Freedom is that quality of existence in which a people recognize their dignity and worth by fighting against the sociopolitical conditions that limit their recognition in society.

Martin King's foremost contribution as a moral thinker was his penetrating insight into the meaning of justice during his time. No one understood justice with more depth or communicated it with greater clarity in the area of race relations in the United States and the world than Martin Luther King, Jr. Because of King, the world is not only more aware of the problem of racial injustice but equally aware of its interrelatedness with poverty and war. "Injustice anywhere is a threat to justice everywhere."[31]

The "anemic democracy" to which King pointed is still present in America and around the world. The dream is still unfulfilled. Whether we speak of the relations between nations or of the relations between persons within nations, the rich few are still getting richer and the poor many are getting poorer. To incorporate the true meaning of Martin Luther King, Jr., into America's national consciousness would mean using our technological resources to bridge the huge economic gap that separates the rich and poor nations.

Martin King's greatest contribution was his ability to communicate a vision of hope in extreme situations of oppression. No matter how difficult the struggle for justice became, no matter how powerful were the opponents of justice, no matter how many people turned against him, King refused absolutely to lose hope, because he believed that ultimately right will triumph over wrong. He communicated that hope to the masses throughout the world, enabling them to keep on struggling for freedom and justice even though the odds were against them.

> I am not going to stop singing "We shall overcome" [he often said], because I know that "truth crushed to the earth shall rise again." I am not going to stop singing "We shall overcome," because I know the Bible is right, "you shall reap what you sow." I am not going to stop singing, "We shall overcome," because I know that one day the God of the

universe will say to those who won't listen to him, "I'm not a playboy. Don't play with me. For I will rise up and break the backbone of your power." I'm not going to stop singing, "We shall overcome," because "mine eyes have seen the glory of the coming of the Lord. He's trampling out the vintage where the grapes of wrath are stored. Glory hallelujah, his truth is marching on."[32]

Demystifying Martin and Malcolm

Martin Luther King, Jr., and Malcolm X evoke contrasting images among most Americans. When people think of Martin King, they usually think of his philosophy of love, nonviolence, and integration—a dream of blacks, whites, and other Americans living and working together in the beloved community. When people think of Malcolm X, they often think of hate, separation, and violence—a nightmare of blacks, whites, and other Americans fighting one another in riot-torn cities. These two contrasting images were created by the mainstream media in the 1960s, and they are still influential today.

When Martin King was assassinated on April 4, 1968, America mourned his tragic death. Prominent government officials acknowledged his great contribution to the nation. President Lyndon Johnson called King an "American martyr," and the U.S. Senate passed a resolution expressing its "appreciation for the immense service and sacrifice of this dedicated American." More than thirty-thousand people attended King's funeral, including eighty members of the U.S. Senate and House of Representatives.

When Malcolm X was assassinated on February 21, 1965, few tears were shed outside of Harlem and America's poorest black neighborhoods. No mainstream media had a kind word to say about him. The *New York Times* called him an "irresponsible demagogue," and *Time* magazine said he was "a disaster to the Civil Rights movement." The black press was not any kinder. They called Malcolm a "professional race baiter" who, as the *Michigan Chronicle* of Detroit put it, "reaped the harvest of his own philosophy." Even black churches did not want to be associated with him. Several churches, including Adam Clayton Powell, Jr.'s Abyssinian Baptist, declined the request to open their doors for Malcolm X's funeral.

Martin King was soon elevated to the status of a national hero. On November 2, 1983, the Congress and President Ronald Reagan established King's birthday as a national public holiday, first observed on January 20, 1986. He is the only American with a holiday in his name alone. By contrast, after Malcolm's death, little attention was paid to him, except among a small group of black nationalists and even smaller number of white and black leftists, who remembered his birthday and assassination.

Recently, however, a strong wind of change began to blow in the African-American community. Many blacks began to question whether the nonviolent, integrationist philosophy of Martin King was adequate for dealing with the economic deprivation of the inner cities and the lack of cultural self-esteem and political power of their inhabitants. Of course, few people deny that the Civil Rights movement enabled blacks to make significant strides toward social and political freedom and equality in America, especially those among the college-educated. There are forty blacks in the U.S. Congress and more than 800 elected public officials throughout the nation. There are more black students and professors in predominantly white colleges and universities, more black lawyers in the big law firms, more black doctors at the major hospitals, and more black professionals in every segment of American society than ever before. Blacks have been "moving on up," to use the theme song of the once popular television sitcom called "The Jeffersons."

But despite the progress in middle-class black America, the black underclass are poorer today than they were in the 1960s. One-half of black babies are born in poverty, and nearly 25 percent of black men between the ages of nineteen and twenty-eight are in jails, prisons, or awaiting their day in court. With no respect for themselves or for anybody else, black youth are dropping out of school, having babies, joining gangs, selling drugs, and killing one another with a frequency that boggles the imagination.

A New Look at Malcolm

Eight years of Ronald Reagan's savage attack upon the black poor shocked the African-American community into taking another look at Malcolm X. Rap musicians and other hip-hop artists, along with Spike Lee's epic movie and the controversy that preceded it, created a resurgence of interest in Malcolm X. "Who is this Malcolm the Tenth?" a black college student asked me, inquiring about my announced lecture and wondering why he had never been told about him. On urban street corners, in college and university classrooms, at conferences and other large community events, on television and radio talk shows, people—particularly younger people—of all races and ethnic groups began talking about Malcolm. A new generation learned of the one-time Harlem hustler and pimp who became the national spokesperson for Elijah Muhammad's Nation of Islam and later an international African-American leader who linked the black freedom struggle in the U.S. with liberation movements in the Third World. Tapes of Malcolm X's speeches are selling well on the streets of inner cities and in music stores. Literature by and about him abounds in bookstores and libraries and is regularly assigned in college and university classes in black studies and other subjects. *The Autobiography of Malcolm X* was on the *New York Times* paperback best-sellers list for nineteen weeks and has appeared on the *Chronicle of Higher Education*'s best-selling list called "What They're Reading on College Campuses."

Malcolm X evokes much more respect today among blacks than he did during his lifetime. In a 1964 *New York Times* poll, only 6 percent named Malcolm as "doing the best work for Negroes." Yesterday's "Negroes" are *black* today. This transformation is reflected in their enhanced appreciation of Malcolm. According to a November, 1992 *Newsweek* poll, 57 percent of all blacks regard Malcolm as a "hero." The younger the respondents, the greater the agreement: a respectable 33 percent among blacks over fifty, but an amazing 84 percent among blacks between fifteen and twenty-four. Young grassroots blacks, alienated from the civil rights organizations and the churches, respect Malcolm like no other person in African-American history. He is an inner city cultural icon who often receives as much devotion from the hip-hop generation as Christians give to Jesus. "Saint Malcolm" is what they sometimes call him. Walking through any big city, one can feel and see the reverence that Malcolm's image evokes. He is a symbol of young blacks' rage against white America's racism and also against middle-class blacks who have forgotten the plight of their poor brothers and sisters left behind in the ghetto.

Malcolm represents an abrasive, "in-your-face" assertion of blackness, a "don't mess with me" attitude. Young blacks love Malcolm's courage to speak the truth that whites did not want to hear. They love his righteous and fearless anger, his eloquence, wit, and self-confidence. Malcolm said in public what most blacks felt but were afraid to say except in private among themselves. He was able to talk defiantly to white people because he did not want anything from them. Here was a black man with only an eighth grade education who, through self-discipline, acquired the intellectual ability to hold his own in debates with black and white scholars. On tee-shirts, sweaters, jackets, and caps, young blacks wear Malcolm's name and face with pride. It is their way of saying, "We are proud to be black like Malcolm, and we don't care who is offended by it." This may sound like a trivial statement to whites, who have never had their identity as human beings seriously questioned. But for young blacks who did not make it in the white man's society and who are told daily by its institutional structures that they are worthless, Malcolm X is a source of inspiration and hope that they can be somebody even in an environment of despair and death.

A Reversal of Places

In contrast to the contemporary "Malcolmania," as one scholar called it, interest in Martin King is declining, especially among young blacks. Martin's vision of the beloved community is sometimes openly denounced as ineffectual, or worse, as complicit with white racism. One does not see caps with K's and not many tee-shirts, sweaters, and jackets with Martin's face and name. He is rarely quoted by rap musicians, and other hip-hop artists seem to pay no attention to him. No epic movie is being planned on Martin's life, and there is little debate about him in the African-American community. Even black college students, who benefit the most from Martin's civil rights work, are more enamored of Malcolm X and black nationalism. From the middle of the 1950s to the middle of the 1980s, Martin King occupied the dominant place in the pantheon of African-American leaders. Among blacks over fifty he still holds that place, but among the young grassroots and college blacks today, the dominant place belongs to Malcolm, with King hardly ever being mentioned.

What are we to make of this reversal of places between Malcolm and Martin? Is it a good or a bad thing for the pendulum to swing toward Malcolm and away from Martin? Anyone who has read my book *Martin & Malcolm & America: A Dream or A Nightmare* or has heard me talk about Martin and Malcolm knows that nothing could please me more than the resurgence of interest in Malcolm X. Uncritical adoration of Martin by both blacks and whites and knee-jerk disparagement of Malcolm have created the false impression that Martin had all the answers and Malcolm had nothing to contribute, or worse, was a hindrance in the black freedom struggle.

Both Martin and Malcolm are needed for a critical understanding of the meaning of America from the vantage point of its inhabitants of African descent. Martin and Malcolm symbolize the two great resistance traditions in black history—integrationism and black nationalism. Who are we? Are we African or American or both? In 1903, the great black scholar W. E. B. Du Bois, in *The Souls of Black Folk*, called the struggle for black identity in America a "peculiar sensation," a "double-consciousness," "two warring ideals in one dark body, whose dogged strength alone keeps it from being torn asunder." Martin and Malcolm together embodied both aspects of the African-American struggle for identity. If we choose one and reject the other, it is like splitting ourselves in half, leading to our certain death. We cannot choose between them and still survive as a healthy people.

What concerns me the most about the resurgence of interest in Malcolm X is that many young blacks are acting as if they do not need Martin King. They are committing the same mistake that their elders made when they ignored Malcolm and exclusively embraced Martin. Civil rights leaders of the 1970s and 1980s gave uncritical praise to Martin's achievements without even acknowledging the contribution of Malcolm. Young blacks are making a similar error today. They rap about Malcolm's profound analysis of America's racism without even mentioning how Martin organized a movement to fight against the racism that Malcolm analyzed. Spike Lee's movie, although a good introduction to the life of Malcolm, makes this same mistake. He portrays Malcolm's life and message without paying sufficient attention to Martin's challenging critique, thereby creating a Malcolm devoid of his complexity. Erring on either side of the mistake, taking Malcolm without Martin or vice versa, is detrimental to black self-understanding. Both mistakes distort the meaning of America for blacks and whites and hide the nature of their struggle to create in America a meaningful life together.

The Radical Martin

Looking at Martin King without sufficient attention to the provocative presence of Malcolm X created an image of King that was primarily defined by and for white America. He is portrayed as the acceptable Negro leader, standing in front of the Lincoln Memorial in 1963, frozen there, looking into the heavens, proclaiming his dream of an America without racial animosity. White people adore the nonviolent "I Have a Dream" Martin, as if he said nothing else about America on that day or afterwards. Without Malcolm's challenging presence, we cannot see clearly the radical Martin, the one who in 1966 to 1968 moved toward Malcolm.

The radical Martin acknowledged that racism was much more deeply embedded in American life than he had initially realized. Many northern whites who supported Martin's campaign against racism in the distant South opposed him when he took the movement to the North and challenged de facto segregation in housing, education, and government. He quit talking about his dream. "I saw that dream turned into a nightmare," he said. Martin declared that there was more racism in Chicago and other northern cities than in Mississippi and the rest of the South. He even acknowledged that "temporary segregation" may be the only way to achieve a genuinely integrated society. He realized, as Malcolm did before him, that tokenism seemed to be the only kind of integration that white people would accept.

The radical Martin was also an anti-war activist and a challenger of the economic order. He called racism, war, and poverty the three great evils of his time. Opposition to the war in Vietnam and to poverty and racism at home and abroad became Martin's major obsession as he proclaimed God's judgment upon America. His opposition was more than just a political protest. It was a theological and prophetic condemnation of America. He had a deep spiritual conviction that the God of the universe is going to establish justice in the world whether America likes it or not. "God is not a playboy," Martin shouted in a sermon, as if he were a biblical prophet, proclaiming God's wrath upon nations that "trample on the needy" and "bring ruin to the poor." "If something doesn't happen soon," Martin said, "I'm convinced that the curtain of doom is coming down on the U.S."

The radical Martin King sounds like Malcolm X. That is why we seldom hear about him during the King holiday celebrations in January. When President Reagan and the Congress established the King holiday, "They voted for Martin's 'I Have a Dream' speech," Andrew Young correctly said. "They didn't vote for his anti-Vietnam speech or his challenge to Lyndon Johnson about ending poverty." Unfortunately, civil rights leaders have done too little to correct the distorted image that whites created for Martin. Putting him in conversation with Malcolm would go a long way toward correcting the distortion.

Malcolm Distorted

Just as Martin King's followers separated him from Malcolm X, thereby allowing his image to be co-opted by white America, Malcolm X's devotees are separating him from Martin, thereby allowing his image to be co-opted by black conservatives and vulgar, dogmatic black nationalists. Malcolm is often portrayed as a black Republican or as a gun-toting black revolutionary. In reality, he was neither. But without an informed, critical portrayal of Malcolm's life and message in dialogue with Martin King and in the historical context of the black freedom struggle of the 1950s and 1960s, Malcolm's image can be manipulated into a point of view he would have despised.

"Was Malcolm X a Republican?" asked Juan Williams, a national correspondent for *The Washington Post.* In an article by that title in the *Gentlemen's Quarterly,* Williams cites several black conservatives who give an affirmative answer. "If Malcolm X were alive today, he would be a black conservative," says Robert L. Woodson, President of National Center for Neighborhood Enterprises. "Everything I do comes right out of Malcolm's playbook." Tony Brown, the TV talk show host, agrees. "I think Malcolm X was essentially a black Republican by today's standards," Brown says. "I use two basic criteria to come to that conclusion. Number one, Malcolm was for individual opportunity. Number two, he was for self-help. This is Republican philosophy. It is right in line with Garvey, Elijah Muhammad, Booker T. Washington, and, most of all, Malcolm X." Even Clarence Thomas, the Supreme Court Justice, claims Malcolm's legacy and can quote him from memory and at length.

What black conservatives are doing in claiming Malcolm X is "proof-texting." Like some people reading the Bible, they select only the passages that support what they already believe. They do not present the complete Malcolm, the one who was critical of white society and of black intellectuals who use their minds to make whites feel better about the crimes they committed against blacks. Black conservatives say what their white counterparts, like Pat Buchanan and Senator Jesse Helms, want to hear, something Malcolm, after his break with the Black Muslims, could never have done. It is true that, as a spokesperson for Elijah Muhammad, Malcolm found himself in conversation with the Ku Klux Klan. That was Elijah Muhammad's Malcolm and not Malcolm thinking for himself. Black conservatives are closer to the philosophy of Elijah Muhammad (who today is represented by Louis Farrakhan) than they are to Malcolm X. Malcolm was a sophisticated international thinker whose philosophy was too political to be contained by the religio-economic philosophy of Elijah Muhammad.

Black conservatives want African-Americans to choose between affirmative action programs (which they reject) and self-help programs (which they embrace), as if the two are contradictory. This is a false choice, and no groups in America are expected to make that choice except blacks and other people of color. Whites do not have to make that choice, especially the men of their group. No group has had more affirmative action programs than they—more than 200 years of them. While blacks were reduced to slavery and Indians were being massacred by the U.S. Army, white men established themselves as the sole rulers of the country and owners of the land. They have doled out privileges to one another as if people of color were not human beings. Only in the last two decades have people been talking about affirmative action programs for blacks, women, and other people of color, and white men have been the first to protest about their rights being denied. The people who took everyone else's rights and never treated any other group as their equal are now claiming that affirmative action programs and entitlements for blacks, women, and other people of color deny them equal justice. Statements like that would not deserve a serious reply but for the fact that they are uttered by the mighty. Such people would not know what true justice means if they saw the Statue of Liberty walking down the street. We need Malcolm X to give us the words to reply to their twisted logic. Malcolm warned blacks about tricky whites who can make the criminal look like the victim and the victim like the criminal. He also warned us about the black intellectuals, who are so interested in being accepted by their white peers that they cannot think in the interest of their community.

Turning to the other distortion of Malcolm, young blacks who separate Malcolm from Martin emphasize his rejection of nonviolence and, by implication, suggest that he advocated violence. But they must be reminded that Malcolm did not carry a gun and never committed an act of violence.

It is interesting to note that Martin, the apostle of nonviolence, did more to create situations of violence between blacks and whites than Malcolm, the so-called prophet of violence. Of course, Malcolm exposed the hypocrisy of whites, who advocated nonviolence for blacks but were not themselves nonviolent. But he did not advocate violence. Malcolm advocated self-defense, the right of blacks to defend themselves when violently attacked by their enemies.

However, even Malcolm's self-defense philosophy was misunderstood. He did not fight whites with guns. He fought them with his intelligence. He contended that the pen was more powerful than the sword. He studied hard so that he could effectively argue the case of blacks in the world court of reason. Malcolm spoke of his debates with white intellectuals as verbal battles, in which the most effective weapons were words, which he called philosophical and theological bullets. He loved to fight with his mind because he believed that he had the truth on his side. He could not wait to do battle with the professors and students at Harvard, Yale, Oxford, and other white institutions of learning. It did not matter what discipline persons represented or who was in the audience, Malcolm was always ready to shape his presentation to what he needed to defeat the opponents of freedom.

Young blacks often fail to grasp the intellectual Malcolm. They are often more interested in "X" clothes and caps than in Malcolm's ideas. Many have not even read his *Autobiography* or any serious commentary on his life and message. They merely cite slogans, like "by any means necessary" as if it were equated with picking up the gun. "Any means," as Malcolm's daughter Attallah Shabazz rightly said, "can involve reading books and studying hard." "Without education," Malcolm warned, "you are not going anywhere in this world."

Young blacks need to get in touch with the intellectual Malcolm and to be transformed by the encounter. To know Malcolm is also to know him in relation to Martin because they were fighting in the same struggle for the same cause. "Dr. King," Malcolm said, "wants the same thing I want— freedom." For both, freedom meant black people affirming their dignity as human beings and demanding that white people treat them accordingly. "If you are not ready to die for it, put the word 'freedom' out of your vocabulary," Malcolm told blacks. Martin told them the same thing: "A [person] who won't die for something is not fit to live." Both Martin and Malcolm did more than just talk about freedom. And they both paid the ultimate price.

Most people who talk about Martin and Malcolm have not studied them, do not know them in the context of their time, and thus cannot assess their meaning for us today. When Supreme Court Justice Clarence Thomas and other black conservatives can claim allegiance to Malcolm and President Ronald Reagan and other white conservatives can claim Martin, then we know that a lot of intellectual work needs to be done so that the true meanings of Martin and Malcolm are not co-opted by their enemies.

Martin was a *political revolutionary*. He transformed the political and social life of black and white Americans. The impact of Martin King's life and message is so profound and widely acknowledged that one hardly needs to make a case for it.

But what about Malcolm X? "What did Malcolm X ever do for the black people," asks Carl T. Rowan, the well-known syndicated black columnist. Both Rowan and Virginia Governor L. Douglas Wilder (now former) agreed with the late Supreme Court Justice Thurgood Marshall, who said that Malcolm never did "one concrete thing" to lift the level of black people's lives and thus "would not miss him if Malcolm had never lived."

It is unfortunate that prominent black professionals are often so blinded by their own success in this society that they cannot see the obvious. Malcolm was a *cultural revolutionary*. He changed the way black people think about themselves. He revolutionized the black mind, transforming docile Negroes and self-effacing colored people into proud blacks and self-confident African-Americans. Both Carl Rowan and Douglas Wilder should acknowledge that Malcolm's legacy created the cultural space for them to be *black* people. They were once Negroes, as most of us were. Even Justice Marshall, the great defender of the political rights of blacks, was transformed from a Negro to an Afro-American. It is unfortunate that he did not acknowledge Malcolm's contribution to his changed identity.

More than anyone else, Malcolm taught blacks that they should be proud of their African origin. "You can't hate the roots of the tree," he said, "and not hate the tree. You can't hate your origin and not end up hating yourself." Malcolm emphasized that the self-confidence to live as free human beings could be achieved only through a people's knowledge of their past. "Just as a tree without roots is dead," he said, "a people without history or cultural roots become a dead people." Malcolm ridiculed blacks who said, "I ain't left nothing in Africa." "Why, you left your mind in Africa," he retorted.

Embracing Martin and Malcolm

Martin and Malcolm embodied in their lives and work the African American struggle for identity in a society that is not sure what to do with us. There is a little bit of Martin and Malcolm in all African-Americans. But many, especially those among the middle class, are reluctant to reveal the Malcolm part of themselves, especially in the presence of whites. They push Malcolm down below their consciousness, sometimes even forgetting that he was ever a part of them.

Most whites are not prepared to listen to the harsh truths of Malcolm X. They like Martin King because, as one white university student said, he "went about everything in the right way," which really means white people's way. Malcolm chose "a more destructive way," which really means a way contrary to the desires of whites. Since Martin spoke a message that appealed to whites, they saw their own image in him and embraced what they saw. That is why they joined with blacks to make King's birthday a national public holiday. There is no possibility that America will bestow the same honor on Malcolm X.

Most whites want blacks to choose Martin over Malcolm, but blacks and other Americans interested in justice should never celebrate Martin without giving equal place to Malcolm. We should not listen to Martin's "I Have a Dream" speech without also listening to Malcolm's answer in his "Message to the Grass Roots." "While King was having a dream," Malcolm said, "the rest of us Negroes are having a nightmare." Without confronting the American nightmare that Malcolm bore witness to, we will never be able to create the beloved community articulated so well by Martin King. How can we overcome racism if we do not admit how deeply this cancer is embedded in American history and culture? Malcolm, not Martin, is the best source for understanding racism and its consequences in America.

But the Afrocentric lovers of Malcolm must be reminded that destroying racism is not the only goal of the struggle for freedom. We blacks must be free not only for ourselves but also for others. On this point, Martin was right, and we must listen to his counsel. "All life is interrelated," he said, "All . . . are caught in an inescapable network of mutuality. Whatever affects one directly affects all indirectly." Neither blacks nor whites or others can be what they ought to be until all realize their full potential.

Blacks must begin with Malcolm, that is, with a healthy regard for themselves—their history and culture as it stretches back to the continent of Africa. But we must not stop with Malcolm. To do so would stunt our growth and thus hinder the realization of our human potential. We must embrace Martin too, as passionately and lovingly as we embrace Malcolm. I know that such a demand will be difficult for many lovers of blackness. But Martin's vision of black people living together with all human beings as brothers and sisters is as important as Malcolm's vision of blacks living together as one. The human family is as important as the black family, because we either learn to live together with others, or we will perish together. We must choose life and not death.

To choose life means to see that racism is not the only contradiction affecting the quality of human life. There are other social evils just as harmful as racism. They include sexism, classism, heterosexism, and the wanton disregard of the earth. Accenting Malcolm's and Martin's critique of racism is not enough. We also must criticize Malcolm and Martin for their failures, especially their blatant sexism, and their silence on homophobia in the black community and the larger society. If we are going to make a new future for ourselves with others, we will need to develop creative and self-critical leadership. We must not deify Martin and Malcolm. They were only human beings with assets and liabilities like all of us. If we do not identify their weaknesses and seek to overcome them, then we will perpetuate them.

Let us, therefore, create an America—not just for Martin and Malcolm, or for whites and blacks but for Latinos, Indians, and Asians and for women in all groups, for gay men and lesbians—for every people, every culture and every faith in this land. When we can do that, we will have achieved the goal for which Martin, Malcolm, and all freedom fighters have struggled.

Going Forward

The church must always be that community of people that is looking for and identifying with those who are voiceless.

—*Enquiry*, March–May, 1971

New Roles in the Ministry:
A Theological Appraisal

Many problems arise concerning the church and its ministry, because we forget what these terms mean in the context of the gospel of Jesus. Aside from the customary verbal confessions of belief in Jesus Christ that we have been conditioned to say in prayers, sermons, and other religious situations, a large number of churchpeople seldom reflect in their everyday lifestyle a faith commitment to the One who was crucified on Golgotha's hill. Our church is an impostor, because we no longer believe the gospel we proclaim. There is a credibility gap between what we say and what we do. While we may preach sermons that affirm the church's interests in the poor and the downtrodden, what we actually do shows that we are committed to the "American way of life," in which the rich are given privileged positions of power in shaping the life and activity of the church, and the poor are virtually ignored. As a rule, the church's behavior toward the poor is very similar to the society at large: The poor are charity cases. Our negligence of them is symbolized in the small offering taken in their name every Sunday morning in most black churches. It is appalling to see some black churches adopting this condescending attitude toward the victims, because these churches were created in order to fight against slavery and injustice. For many slaves, the Black Church was God's visible instrument for freedom and justice. Therefore, to have contemporary middle-class black Christians treating the poor as second-class members of the church is a disgrace not only to the Scripture but also to our black religious heritage.

Because our churches adopt their value system from the American capitalistic society and not from Jesus Christ, church offices are more often than not valued as indications that one has achieved a certain status in life. This partly accounts for the fact that women are not permitted in any denomination to exercise power commensurate with their numbers, and

111

in some denominations are even denied ordination. Although there is room for legitimate debate in these matters, it seems clear that no appeal to Scripture or church tradition can remove the suspicion that all who stand against the equality of women in every dimension of the Church's life do so in the light of the political and social interests of men. Whatever the exegesis of Scripture and tradition one may advocate, one fact is certain: When a particular interpretation of Scripture benefits people who hold positions of power, it can never be the gospel of Jesus.

No amount of clever reasoning can camouflage the obvious social, economic, and political interests involved in the subordination of women in the church. Black women know that their ministry has been severely limited, and they also know why. That is, they know *who* benefits from their oppression. That is the reason they now openly speak of "new roles in the ministry." Such a theme is not only appropriate, but necessary, so that attention can be called to certain apostasies and heresies in the Black Church.

The need for a definition of new roles for women and men in the Black Church arises not from the fact that the gospel is new or is changing. The opposite is the case: There is a *constancy* about the gospel that is derived from the One who is the content of its message. Anyone who encounters the biblical God experiences the divine constancy. In the Scriptures, God's constancy is spoken of as divine faithfulness, that is, God's promise to be with and for the people in time of trouble. Theologians of the early church, paying more attention to Greek philosophy than to the Bible, spoke of the divine constancy in terms of the absence of suffering in the Being of God. But more than one thousand years later, black slaves took the tradition *back* to the Scriptures by expressing their confidence in a divine constancy that was clearly derived from biblical roots.

> *God is a God!*
> *God don't never change!*
> *God is a God*
> *An' He always will be God.*

This constancy was the foundation of their faith and the source of black slaves' confidence that God had not left them alone in servitude. In this essay I want to examine the idea of new roles in the ministry for black men and women in the light of the constancy of the gospel of Jesus.

The Holy Spirit and Social Reality

One of the most important and perplexing questions in systematic theology is the relation between the gospel and culture. What is this gospel that does not change? What is it that we preach and sing about that is the same today as yesterday and will be the same tomorrow and forevermore? Unless we answer this question, then there is no way to identify the new roles that our ministry is required to take in our faithfulness to the gospel of Jesus. By failing to identify the universal dimension of the gospel and to subject it to the judgment of Scripture and the traditions of the church, we leave ourselves vulnerable to the charge of ideology, that is, allowing the gospel to be defined by our cultural and political interests. While I do not agree with Karl Barth's assertion that there is an "infinite qualitative distinction" between God and humanity, it is still true that we seek a Christian lifestyle and proclamation that are not simply the values of our society or community. This means that we must ask the critical question, "What is the gospel, and how is it different from my own social conditioning?"

However, before we can define the gospel and then develop new roles in the ministry on the basis of its proclamation, it is necessary to describe the theological and social context in which my perspective on the gospel has been shaped. I do not believe that it is possible to understand what the gospel is all about in terms of its demands on people in our world unless one encounters the Spirit, that is, God's presence with the people. The Spirit refers to God's gift of the power of insight so that one can hear and do the truth as revealed in the biblical witness. Without an openness to the power and guidance of the divine Spirit and her presence in the world, we will not understand what the gospel is. One should not belittle the value of disciplined intellectual effort in the life of the church, but the gospel is more than intellectual study. Sometimes intellectual formulations give us a false confidence about our understanding of the truth. This has often been the case with the literary and historical criticism of the Bible. The truth of the Bible is simply not accessible apart from the Spirit.

To claim that the Spirit is needed to understand what the gospel is, is to say that our resources alone are not enough to know who Jesus is. To speak of Jesus and his gospel is to speak of his Spirit who opens up dimensions of reality that are not reducible to our intellectual capacity. The Spirit is the power to hear and do the truth as lived by the people. Without an openness to walk and talk with Jesus and to be led by a Spirit not of our own creation, there is no way to hear the gospel and to live out its meaning in our ministry.

But lest we think that God's Spirit is merely a pious feeling in our hearts, it is necessary to point out the relations between social reality and God's presence in the world. The only way to encounter God's Spirit is to have one's religious consciousness formed in a political context. The social and political context of the victims is indispensable for hearing our true calling, a vocation that is always bound up with the liberation of victims from servitude. It is not possible for anyone to hear the divine Spirit's call into the Christian ministry, and at the same time derive his or her perception of that ministry from an ecclesiastical structure that oppresses women.

One does not need a seminary education to know that oppression in any form is a contradiction of God's Spirit. Indeed, I firmly believe that the insight into the radical contradiction between the divine Spirit and human oppression is disclosed to people only when they find their consciousness being formed in a community of victims. There will be no new roles in the ministry for women and men unless they are created in the struggle of freedom for the victims of the land. We do not learn this insight in seminaries, because they are largely defined by the existing structures of power. We may hear about Marx, Fanon, and Gutiérrez in white seminaries, but we must not mistake revolutionary rhetoric for actual praxis in the community of victims. Rhetoric is learned in the classrooms by reading Marx's *Das Kapital* and Fanon's *Wretched of the Earth*. But if we are to take Marx seriously when he says, "It is not consciousness that determines life but life that determines consciousness," then we must conclude that a true revolutionary consciousness is formed only in the social context of victims. Only as we join the poor in their struggle can we encounter the divine Spirit of liberation disclosed in their fight for justice.

The Gospel Defined

What is this gospel that can only be understood in the social and political context of victims and from which new styles of ministry must be shaped in the Black Church? I do not want to spend too much time repeating what I have written and said elsewhere. Yet I will say something about defining the gospel, partly to avoid being misunderstood, but more because I come from that tradition of black preachers who contended that one should never pass up an opportunity to say a word about Jesus. Therefore I am compelled by the nature of my vocation to say a word about what we call the "gospel of Jesus."

To put it as clearly as I know how: *The Christian gospel is God's good news to the victims that their humanity is not determined by their victimization.* This means that the poor do not have to adjust to poverty; the oppressed do not have to reconcile themselves to humiliation and suffering. They can do something to change not only their perception of themselves, but also the existing structures of oppression. Indeed, this is what the Exodus, the prophets, and the Incarnation are all about. These events and people are God's way of saying that injustice is a contradiction of the divine intention of humanity. Persons, therefore, who embark on a vocation in the Christian ministry and do not view their calling as a commitment to the victims of the land are not really servants of the gospel of Jesus. We may be servants of the United Methodist or A.M.E. denominations, but not of the One whom the Lucan Evangelist reported as saying:

> The Spirit of the Lord is upon me
> because he has anointed me to preach good news to the poor.
> He has sent me to proclaim release to the captives
> and recovering of sight to the blind,
> to set at liberty those who are oppressed,
> to proclaim the acceptable year of the Lord.
>
> *(Luke 4:18–19)*

Jesus' consciousness was defined by his identity with the liberation of the weak and helpless. That is why the Lucan account tells us that he was born in a stable at Bethlehem. We are also told that Jesus defined his ministry for the poor and not the rich. Jesus' identity with the victims led to his condemnation as a criminal of the Roman State. If Jesus had been born in the emperor's court and had spent most of his life defending the interests of the rulers of that court, then what I am saying would have no validity at all. It is because the Scripture is so decisively clear on this matter that I insist on the liberation of the victim from social and economic oppression as the heart of the gospel. Anything less than this message is an ideological distortion of the biblical message.

Therefore, whatever new styles we create, they must never be allowed to camouflage the true meaning of the gospel. Our endeavor to "get with it," to be "up-to-date" or avant-garde must never deter us from our calling.

I like being fashionable as much as anybody else. There is nothing wrong with that, if it does not become a substitute for the substance of our faith. This faith is universal and is identical with God's will to liberate the victims of the land.

To go further, not only must the new styles not obscure the gospel, they must actually be derived from the gospel. Otherwise we run the risk of having our ministry controlled by another Lord. This is the danger of every theological movement. Whether one speaks of the old or new quest of the historical Jesus, liberalism or neo-orthodoxy, secular theology or liberation theologies among Latin Americans, white women, or black people, we must never forget the basic proclamation and praxis that make the gospel *the* gospel in our cultural and political settings.

Whatever we do at Garrett-Evangelical, or Union and Yale, we must not forget about the faith of our mothers and fathers. For it was this faith that enabled our grandparents to survive the slave ships and a lifetime of servitude in North America. Not much has been written about their faith, since they were not white and thus not privileged to learn to read and write theological discourses. Instead, we read about their enslavers and the theological justifications they made in defense of white supremacy and American domination. Of course, the validity of the faith of our mothers and fathers must not be determined by theological criteria devised by the descendents of slave masters. Rather, the authenticity of our parents' faith should be decided by whether or not that faith empowered them to live as they sang. They sang that Jesus is a "bridge over troubled water," that he is the "lily of the valley and the bright and morning star." To test the validity of these faith claims is to ask whether our parents gave up in despair in slavery and oppression or whether they continued to fight in the knowledge and hope that oppressors did not have the last word about their humanity. I think the historical record speaks for itself. We have been bequeathed a faith that brought our grandparents through hard trials and great tribulations. Therefore we should not abandon it in our search of new lifestyles in the ministry. Since this faith has survived the tests of slavery, lynchings, and ghettos and has sustained our parents in their struggle to be something other than what white people said they were, we black heirs of this faith should not be too quick to discard the religion of our ancestors. I believe that we ought to follow unashamedly in their footsteps and sing as they once sang:

> *Give me that old-time religion,*
> *Give me that old-time religion,*
> *Give me that old-time religion,*
> *It's good enough for me.*

The epistemological reason for our confidence in that "old-time religion" is grounded in our claim that "it was good enough for our mothers," and "it was tried in the fiery furnace." Therefore, "it's good enough for you and me." Our parents also claimed that "it will make you love everybody," and "will do when you are dying." This religion must be the source for our definition of new roles in the ministry.

New Roles in the Ministry: Black Women and Men

What are these new roles that are required for the Church to remain faithful to the gospel of Jesus expressed in black people's old-time religion? To answer the question, I would like to say a word about new roles in the Black Church for women and men. For obvious reasons, this is not an easy subject for me to talk about in that I, like most, have been socially conditioned to accept what white culture has defined as the woman's place in the church and society. And even though I may assert the liberation of black women, that public assertion alone is no guarantee that I truly share the commitment that black women should not be oppressed by anybody, including black male clergy. But regardless of the question that may remain about the validity of my conversion, the gospel is quite clear on this matter. The gospel bears witness to the God who is against oppression in any form, whether inflicted on an oppressed group from the outside or arising from within an oppressed community. The Exodus is the prime example of the first instance, and the rise of prophecy is a prominent example of the second. But in both cases, Yahweh leaves no doubt that oppression is not to be tolerated. Therefore, people who claim to believe in the biblical God and also claim that this God supports the subordination of women to men have not really understood the Bible. They have distorted it and thus confused cultural limitations and errors with the message itself.

If the biblical message is one of liberation, then a ministry based on that message must be creative and liberating. There is no place for differences in the roles of men and women in the ministry. God has created man and woman as equals, that is, as co-partners in service of freedom. Therefore, whatever differences are found in present-day churches arise from human sin, that is, the will of men to dominate and control women. If we are to be true ministers of the gospel, then we must create new roles for everyone so that the distinctions between man and woman for the purpose of domination are no longer a reality for our churches. We must liberate our own community from its own internal destructiveness, so that we will be free to fight against oppression in the larger society.

It is a contradiction for black men to protest against racism in the white church and society at large and then fail to apply the same critique to themselves in their relation to black women. This contradiction led Sister Frances Beale to comment that the black man "sees the system for what it is for the most part, but where he rejects its values on many issues, when it comes to women, he seems to take his guidelines from the pages of the *Ladies Home Journal.*"[1]

If black people are going to create new roles in the ministry, black men will have to recognize that the present status of black women in the ministry is not acceptable. Since the gospel is about liberation, it demands that we create structures of human relations that enhance freedom and not oppression.

I know that such affirmations are more easily said than done. Where then do we begin? Liberation is not an individual's agenda but, rather, the commitment of the black community. If we black men and women shall achieve freedom, we must do it together. Accordingly, the test of the authenticity of our commitment to freedom is found not only in what we say about freedom generally, but in what we do about the liberation of victims within our community. We cannot support a subordinate ministry for women and also claim to be for the liberation of the oppressed. How is black men's insistence on the subordination of black women in the church and society any different from white people's enforcement of black subordination? No matter how much we wish the similarity to be nonexistent, it is unmistakably present. This point has been clearly stated by Anna Hedgman:

> We have had the extra burden of being women. But if you just review
> the problems that women face, you need only substitute the word

Afro-American people for the word women and you have the same
problems—job discrimination, want ads that discriminate, and false
stereotypes.[2]

Moreover, when the heat has cooled and the dust has cleared in the black
man and woman debate, the black male's arguments against authentic female empowerment, as defined from the black woman's perspective, are
virtually the same as the white racist arguments against black people. The
similarity of the arguments should at least be enough to cause black men
to question heretofore accepted dogma about the secondary role that has
been created for women in the Black Church.

I think the time has come for black men and women to create new roles
in the ministry so that the church can better serve as a liberating agent in
the community. But the question is, Where do we look for role models in
the ministry? Who will provide the resources that we will use for the definition of our ministry? Where will we turn for inspiration, that is, for images that will shape our perceptions of ourselves and what our ministry
ought to be? We could say the gospel of Jesus, but that is too easy and consequently does not reflect sufficiently the ambiguity of the relation between culture and the gospel. There is no gospel that is not at the same
time related to politics and culture. Therefore whatever we may say about
the otherness in the gospel, we cannot avoid asking what cultural and historical resources we will use to organize our perceptions and images of the
Christian ministry. Will we turn to Europe or Africa, to white American
Christianity or to the black religious tradition?

This question is especially applicable to black men whose definition of
ministry in relation to women appears to be derived from white church
traditions. If our definitions of the ministry are uncritically derived from
people who have systematically tried to oppress us, is it not reasonable to
conclude that we ought to be suspicious of their models of the ministry? If
our perception of the woman's place in the ministry is derived from beliefs
and doctrines concocted by people who enslaved our grandparents, how
do we know that their doctrines about the woman's place are not inti-
mately connected with their beliefs concerning black people's place? Is it
not possible that the two doctrines are derived from the same root disease?
This does not necessarily mean that the struggles of white women are
identical with black people's liberation. It does mean that oppressions are

interconnected, and if black men are incapable of self-criticism, we will be guilty of the same crimes against our women as white men are against theirs.

I believe that the resources for our creation of new roles must come from our own tradition. Whatever we may think about the difficulties of male-female relations in the black community, we know that we have a common heritage, which reaches back to our African homeland. We are an African people; we cannot affirm that too often, because we live in a land where people try to make us believe that we have no identity except what is given by white oppressors. Both black women and men were stolen from Africa and brought on ships in chains to the shores of the Americas. Both were made to work in the fields from sun-up to nightfall. No distinctions were made between black men and women in relation to the brutality meted out in slavery. A Gullah woman's comment is graphic and to the point: "Ah done been in sorrow's kitchen and ah licked de pots clean."

But despite white brutality, we have not been destroyed or defeated. We still believe that "we shall overcome." This hope is not a "pie-in-the-sky" religion, but the religion of our grandparents who tested it in the cotton fields of Arkansas, Alabama, and Mississippi. If we create new roles in the ministry on the basis of this religion, there will be no place for those who want to oppress their sisters. We need all the strength, courage, and power that we can get in order to fight against the principalities and powers of this world.

Therefore we conclude with an appeal to black sisters and brothers in the church: The time has come for us to deal honestly with our differences, our hurts, and our pains. We cannot pretend any longer that all is well and that the problem of male-female relations is limited to the white community. It is in the black community as well; and it is time that we face up to the need to speak openly and frankly about what is right and wrong in our community in relation to black men and women. We must continue the hard task of healing the wounds that we inflict on one another. For it is only as we build strong and healing relationships with each other that we are then given the strength and courage to "keep on keeping on" until freedom comes for all humankind.

Black Theology and the
Black College Student

B lack religion and theology are not popular subjects among young blacks, especially those who attend white colleges and universities. Most university blacks are alienated from the religion of their mothers and fathers, and, like their white counterparts, often identify religion as the opiate of the people. Sometimes young black students uncritically equate black religion with white Christianity and thus contend that all talk about Jesus and God, so dominant in black churches, must cease if black people are going to liberate themselves from the values that enslaved them. During the sixties and early seventies it was not uncommon to hear young black radicals proclaim that "Christianity is the white man's religion, and it must be destroyed along with white oppressors." When they did appeal to religion in their articulation of black consciousness, they embraced Islam or African Traditional Religions rather than Christianity. The assumption was that nothing white could liberate black people from a bondage created and perpetrated by whites. Black Christianity was also rejected, because it was regarded as the defender of the white values of American life and culture.

An illustration of this attitude toward black Christianity was found at the Congress of African People (CAP), held in Atlanta, Georgia, in 1970. At that time, CAP was thoroughly nationalist under the leadership of Amiri Baraka (LeRoi Jones). I was asked by Baraka to lead the religion workshop, because he had been impressed by my book *Black Theology and Black Power.* I will never forget that meeting. Many participants contended that we are an African people and that that continent will be the source of our liberation. There were about one hundred people in my workshop and nearly as many views on religion. Each person was sure that he or she had the whole truth and nothing but the truth, and any deviation from the party line was interpreted as heresy or apostasy. Needless to say, there were many heresy battles between the various viewpoints expressed. I spent most of my time trying to referee so that the discussion would stay at a level of mutual respect of opposing views. But all participants agreed that Christianity was the white man's religion, and that it deserved no status in an African Congress. I felt very uneasy with denunciations of black Christianity, because I was a *Christian* theologian and a preacher. From childhood I had come to know the Black Church as an instrument of survival and liberation in my community. Therefore, when these young blacks, who appeared to know very little about the past and present reality of the Black Church, began to denounce the God of my parents and grandparents, I wanted to challenge the authenticity of their denunciations.

I began to think about the function of religion in black life and the role it has played in the affirmation of black humanity. The same religion these young blacks were denouncing has been the source of black people's hope that "trouble won't last always." The particularity of that hope was expressed every time the people made their stand against white structures that attempted to delimit black humanity. In a personal manner, this hope was concretized when my father made his stand against the white folks of Bearden. The year was 1954. Whites had declared that they were going to lynch Charlie Cone because he refused to withdraw his name from a legal school case. I can remember my father's defiant response: "Let the sons of bitches come, they may get me, but they can be sure that I will take some of them with me." He stayed up all night waiting, but they never came. His courage to stand was derived from the very source that these young blacks in Atlanta were denying.

How was it possible for one to grow up black in America and not be aware of the spiritual sources of strength and courage in black culture and history? This was my question as I tried to reconcile the apparent contradictions between the faith of the young university student and the mature Black Church member. It appeared that the young had grown up without any knowledge of the faith of their parents and were thus cut off from the true origin of their struggle.

I can remember clearly my father's contention that he could stand against white folks and the evil they represented because God was standing with him. Other black people of Macedonia made the same faith affirmation. That was why they shouted and prayed so passionately on Sunday morning. Contrary to the popular opinion on college and university campuses, Black Church worship is not primarily compensatory or otherworldly in any negative sense. Black Church worship was born in the struggle of the people to affirm worth in their lives and not to let personhood be destroyed by white people. This is what the black folks of Macedonia meant when they sang:

> Through the years I kept on toiling.
> Toiling through the storm and rain.
> Patiently, waiting and watching till
> my Savior comes again.
> I am comin' Lord,
> Trustin' in your word.
> Keep me from the path of sin;
> Hide me in thy love,
> Write my name above.
> O when the gates swings open,
> I'll go walkin' in.

The very presence of the people together meant that God had given them a little more strength and courage to fight until freedom comes. The people's singing and preaching was not primarily an outward display of piety but an acknowledgment of the felt presence of God in their midst, "buildin' them up where they are torn down and proppin' them up on every leanin' side." The songs of Zion always took on an added meaning in the context of an immediate crisis as with my father. When a brother or a sister was in trouble, the people put a little extra passion and soul into their songs and prayers in order to express their solidarity with the one in trouble. Their religious expressions also confirmed their confidence that God does not leave the little ones alone in a world full of trouble. In situations of extreme suffering, as is so often the case in black life, the people turn to God as that *other* reality who places an indelible stamp of humanity on their being. That is the meaning of the song:

> Without God I could do nothing;
> Without God my life would fail;
> Without God my life would be rugged;
> Just like a ship without a sail.

It is an interesting and sad contradiction that many nationalists of the sixties and seventies had little or no place for their elders in the struggle. The struggle was almost exclusively youth-oriented, a very un-African way to run a revolution. And perhaps that is why the revolution had very little staying power. It had no roots in the culture of our ancestors. I think that the lack of staying power of most so-called radicals, of whatever revolutionary persuasion, is due to their failure to ground the struggle in the life and culture of the *people*. We may claim that we do but our actions betray what we say. Most of us are too busy being black, African, or whatever recent term we select as the "in" word than to care about our people. The absence of radical blacks in the Black Church is all the evidence needed to show that they do not mean what they say.

The rejection of Christianity by young blacks is not simply a nationalist phenomenon or simply an event of the past. It is found today in many college and university settings. Many young black college students, especially on white campuses, dismiss Christianity and the Black Church on intellectual grounds. They tend to identify both with a lack of intelligence. They view the Black Church as the place where unintelligent blacks go to sing and shout about another world, because they cannot do anything to change this world. I have lectured at more than 150 colleges and universities in the United States and have taught in the North, South, East, and West. I think it is fair to say that I have been exposed to a broad range of what black college students think about religion. One thing is sure: Black religion is not a popular course of study among blacks in academic circles.

Another way of noting the rejection of black Christianity and the Black Church is to notice their absence in most Black Studies programs. Black Studies have been known to offer courses ranging from "cornbread and black-eye peas" to the most remote kingdoms in African history, all of which have their place and validity in an appropriate context. But seldom does one find courses dealing with the historical and contemporary Black Church in a positive and creative manner. How is it possible to deal with the center of the black experience and history, however they might be defined, without coming to terms with the most visible faith of the people? How is it possible to tell our story without Richard Allen, James Varick, and Henry McNeal Turner? How can we really understand Harriet Tubman and Sojourner Truth without probing the faith that they claim held them together for struggle? How can we say we are leading a struggle of, for, and by the people when we have no knowledge of, nor respect for, the Jesus they claimed "picked them up, turned them around, and placed their feet on solid ground?" Even if we cannot hold the faith they affirm, are we not at least obliged to respect their faith if we expect to understand why the people regard it as the only source of their survival?

I am the first to admit that there is much validity for this young black critique of the Black Church. There are pimps in religion as there are on the streets in the black community. Far too many black preachers are more concerned about their personal interests than they are about the liberation of black people from white political oppression. Far too many church people are more concerned about erecting a new church building than they are about building a new black community so that all black children will have a more humane place in which to live. I do not deny that many black churches contradict what they claim to affirm. One could spend hours and days talking about the shortcomings of the Black Church. So let us admit that it is a black middle-class institution that tends to reflect the values of white America. Then why should anyone be concerned about the absence of young blacks in the church and especially a black liberation theologian?

There are several responses to this question. First of all, my difficulty with young college and university blacks who rejected black Christianity and the church was their failure to apply their logic in other contexts. If the Black Church reflects white values, then so do the universities, hospitals, legal institutions, and other aspects of black life of which these radicals avail themselves, but with no apparent contradictions in their consciousness. Practically every institution in America is white. Indeed, the institution that is perhaps least white in terms of actual control is the very one that many radical blacks rejected. Why did these ultra-black revolutionaries reject a black institution? Such a question was almost impossible to ask. Black radicals were concerned about revolution, not discussion, understandably so, because the pain of black life was and is an ever present reality. People get tired of talking about alternatives when blood is flowing in the streets. Black radicals were not about to discuss alternatives with black preachers whom they sometimes accurately identified with passivity. When David Hilliard, then chairman of the Black Panther Party, spoke at the annual convention of the National Committee of Black Churchmen in Oakland (1969), his comment to black preachers was: "You are the enemy unless you are ready to pick up the gun and shoot the pigs." There was no dialogue. Hilliard had all the answers, black preachers were at best questionable allies, and he was simply testing out that possibility.

While I can understand black radicals' impatience with the church during and after that period, we still must ask, what function does the criticism have? Does it bring us together for struggle or does it separate us into the "good" and the "bad," as if there are no contradictions among the so-called radicals and the educated. Every black person lives a life full of contradictions, but the greatest contradiction of all is to pretend that they are absent. The critique we apply to the church and its preachers ought to be applied to ourselves as well. For self-criticism is the beginning of wisdom. What we claim to be wrong with the Black Church is also wrong in other professional and institutional contexts. The task, then, is not to be destructive in our critique of the Black Church but creative so that the church can become what it was created to be: the liberating agent of the oppressed of the land.

My second response is directed toward the tendency of young university blacks to let white people define what Christianity or black religion is. The power of definition is the key to one's ability to control one's future and thus one's perception of the self. If white people are allowed to define what is going on in our community, then they can enslave us mentally. They can tell us who we are, and we will believe it.

Unfortunately, most young blacks do not recognize that what they think about the Black Church is often determined by what whites have taught them to believe. One can hardly doubt that there is a connection between the education in white institutions and alienation from one's roots in the black community. When one studies in white institutions from fourteen to twenty years, reading about white Western civilization, one cannot emerge from that brainwashing experience without being affected at the center of one's consciousness. The one institution that still shows a measure of black consciousness and control is the Black Church, and the extent of black alienation from the church in the university shows how much white people have succeeded in dividing our community. One thing is certain: If we are to be liberated, we will have to do it *together*. The oppressor knows that. Therefore, much of his strategy is designed to separate us so that we will fight among ourselves rather than against the oppressive structures that dehumanize us.

I hope the young university blacks will realize this and thus find their way back into the church. For I must admit that I cannot support any revolution that excludes my mother, and she believes in Jesus. She claims that "when you are in trouble and burdened with care and don't know what to do, take it to Jesus and he will fix it for you. He will lift your burdens and ease your pain. Jesus," she contends, "can do most anything." Now I know this testimony will not go over big with young blacks whose theoretical frame is derived from white educational institutions. But if we believe that white oppressors will not provide the means of black liberation, then we had better become suspicious of what is happening to black consciousness in white educational contexts. It could be that our freedom is not found in Karl Marx or any black facsimile thereof, but in the shouts and moans in the black experience. If freedom is found in our experience, it must have something to do with the triumph of the weak over the strong. This is the theme of black folklore with Br'er Rabbit, High John the Conquerer, and Stagolee. This same theme is found in the songs and sermons of black people. Is it possible that our freedom is found here in black life and culture and nowhere else? This is certainly the belief of the Black Church.

Most university blacks have a distorted view of the Black Church. They think of it too superficially, as if all that preaching and shouting are nothing but a reflection of black people's passive acceptance of their oppression. Sometimes this is true, of course; the exciting fact is that sometimes it is not. The black struggle for freedom was born in the church and has always had religious overtones. We must not forget that Nat Turner was a Baptist preacher. It was the Reverend Henry H. Garnett, a Presbyterian minister, who urged slaves in 1843 to demand their freedom, because liberty was a gift from God. The same biblical theme was present in David Walker's *Appeal*. It was Bishop Henry M. Turner who, in 1898, said that "God is a Negro," thereby separating black religion from white religion and connecting the AME Church with the black struggle of freedom. Whatever we might think about Adam Clayton Powell, Jr., and Martin Luther King, Jr., we must not forget their contribution to our struggle. Both connected their struggle with the Black Church and with Jesus' claim that he came to set at liberty those who were oppressed. When we look at the history of the Black Church as told in Gayraud Wilmore's *Black Religion and Black Radicalism*, there are many shortcomings and failures. But there is also the constant theme of liberation and God's will to establish justice in the land.

Let us return momentarily to the situation of slavery. We must not forget that slavery was brutal and cruel and not every black could expect to escape from its oppressive structures. Not every black could buy his freedom or run away in the night. What is a people to do when there are so few concrete possibilities for the affirmation of their humanity? When the existing societal structures define them as nobody, how are they to know that they are somebody? Must their humanity always depend upon their willingness to fight politically against impossible odds as if the affirmation of their somebodiness depends upon their willingness to commit suicide? Must every black take Nat Turner's option in order to affirm his humanity? I do not think so.

Black religion and theology provided additional options for black slaves to fight for freedom in history without being determined by their historical limitations. This is what the concept of heaven means in the slave songs and sermons. Heaven was not so much a cosmological description of the next world as it was a theological affirmation that black humanity cannot be defined by what white people do to our physical bodies. Whites may enslave us and define Africans as savages, but the words of slavemasters do not have to be taken seriously when we know that we have a heavenly Father who cares about his own.

In the midst of political economic disfranchisement, black slaves held themselves together and did not lose their spiritual composure because they believed that their worth transcended governmental decisions. That was why they looked forward to "walking in Jerusalem just like John" and longed for the "camp meeting in the Promised Land."

I know that some blacks will be suspicious of the so-called political implications of the slave songs and sermons that emphasized heaven. They have been taught so much about the opiate character of heaven that it is hard for them to see any political significance in the term. Frederick Douglass's claim about double-meaning notwithstanding, heaven-talk for many blacks is a sign of weakness and passivity. I do not want to debate this point because there is evidence on both sides, and it is not my intention to show that black Christianity is the whole truth and nothing but the truth. But we must ask about present alternatives and their *sources*. Do we have alternatives that are more meaningful than the struggles of our grandparents? If we do, then where do they come from?

My contention is simply this: black religion does not have to be, and often is not, the opiate of the people. If we believe that our struggle is dependent on the majority of black people and not on an intellectual elite, then we must go where the masses are—the church. No one speaks to as many people on a regular basis as the black preacher. Anyone who claims to be for the liberation of the people and yet remains separated from their religious hopes and dreams is a liar. To be for the people is to be united with them in their struggle to realize on earth what they have seen in heaven. We must not play intellectual games with the people's conception of their struggle. Rather, we must get down with them and feel what they feel so that we, like they, will know that "we'll soon be free." This freedom, about which the people prayed and preached, is not a pious feeling in the heart. Freedom is a struggle wrought out of the blood and tears of our mothers and fathers. It is a risk derived from the conviction that death is preferable to life in servitude.

White Theology Revisited

> Are doctors of divinity blind, or are they hypocrites? I suppose some are the one, and some the other, but I think if they felt the interest in the poor and the lowly, that they ought to feel, they would not be so *easily* blinded.
>
> Linda Brent [Harriet Jacobs], *Incidents in the Life of a Slave Girl*, [1861] 1973

People often ask me whether I am still angry as when I wrote *Black Theology and Black Power*. When I hear that question I smile to contain my rage: I remain just as angry because America, when viewed from the perspective of the black poor, is no closer to Martin Luther King, Jr.'s dream of a just society than when he was killed. While the black middle class has made considerable economic progress, the underclass, despite America's robust economy, is worse off in 1998 than in 1968. The statistics are well known, yet they still fail to shock or outrage most Americans.

America is still two societies: one rich and middle-class and the other poor and working-class. William J. Wilson called the underclass "the truly disadvantaged,"[1] people with few skills to enable them to compete in this technological, informational age. To recognize the plight of the poor does not require academic dissection. It requires only a drive into the central cities of the nation to see people living in places not fit for human habitation.

 What deepens my anger today is the appalling silence of white theologians on racism in the United States and the modern world. Whereas this silence has been partly broken in several secular disciplines, theology remains virtually mute. From Jonathan Edwards to Walter Rauschenbusch and Reinhold Niebuhr to the present, progressive white theologians, with few exceptions, write and teach as if they do not need to address the radical contradiction that racism creates for Christian theology. They do not write about slavery, colonialism, segregation, and the profound cultural link these horrible crimes created between white supremacy and Christianity. The cultural bond between European values and Christian beliefs is so deeply woven into the American psyche and thought process that their identification is assumed. White images and ideas dominate the religious life of Christians and the intellectual life of theologians, reinforcing the "moral" right of white people to dominate people of color economically and politically. White supremacy is so widespread that it becomes a "natural" way of viewing the world. We must ask therefore: Is racism so deeply embedded in Euro-American history and culture that it is impossible to do theology without being antiblack?

There is historical precedent for such ideological questioning. After the Jewish Holocaust, Christian theologians were forced to ask whether anti-Judaism was so deeply woven into the core of the gospel and Western history that theology was no longer possible without being anti-Semitic? Recently feminists asked an equally radical question, whether patriarchy was so deeply rooted in biblical faith and its male theological tradition that one could not do Christian theology without justifying the oppression of women. Gay and lesbian theologians are following the feminist lead and are asking whether homophobia is an inherent part of biblical faith. And finally, Third World theologians, particularly in Latin America, forced many progressive First World theologians to revisit Marx's class critique of religion or run the risk of making Christianity a tool for exploiting the poor.

Race criticism is just as crucial for the integrity of Christian theology as any critique in the modern world. Christianity was blatantly used to justify slavery, colonialism, and segregation for nearly five hundred years. Yet this great contradiction is consistently neglected by the same white male theologians who would never ignore the problem that critical reason poses for faith in a secular world. They still do theology as if white supremacy created no serious problem for Christian belief. Their silence on race is so conspicuous that I sometimes wonder why they are not greatly embarrassed by it.

How do we account for such a long history of white theological blindness to racism and its brutal impact on the lives of African people? Is it because white theologians do not know about the tortured history of the Atlantic slave trade, which, according to British historian Basil Davidson, "cost Africa at least fifty million souls"?[2] Have they forgotten about the unspeakable crimes of colonialism? Author Eduardo Galeano claims that 150 years of Spanish and Portuguese colonization in Central and South America reduced the indigenous population from 90 million to 3.3 million.[3] During the twenty-three-year reign of terror of King Leopold II of

Belgium in the Congo (1885–1908), scholarly estimates suggest that approximately 10 million Congolese met unnatural deaths—"fully half of the territory's population."[4] The tentacles of white supremacy have stretched around the globe. No people of color have been able to escape its cultural, political, and economic domination.

Two hundred forty-four years of slavery and one hundred years of legal segregation, augmented by a reign of white terror that lynched more than five thousand blacks, defined the meaning of America as "white over black."[5] White supremacy shaped the social, political, economic, cultural, and religious ethos in the churches, the academy, and the broader society. Seminary and divinity school professors contributed to America's white nationalist perspective by openly advocating the superiority of the white race over all others. The highly regarded church historian Philip Schaff of Union Seminary in New York (1870–1893) spoke for most white theologians in the nineteenth century when he said: "The Anglo-Saxon and Anglo-American, of all modern races, possess the strongest national character and the one best fitted for universal dominion."[6]

Present-day white theologians do not express their racist views as blatantly as Philip Schaff. They do not even speak of the "Negro's cultural backwardness," as America's best known social ethicist, Reinhold Niebuhr, often did and as late as 1965.[7] To speak as Schaff and Niebuhr spoke would be politically incorrect in this era of multiculturalism and color blindness. But that does not mean that today's white theologians are less racist. It only means that their racism is concealed or unconscious. As long as religion scholars do not engage racism in their intellectual work, we can be sure that they are as racist as their grandparents, whether they know it or not. By not engaging America's unspeakable crimes against black people, white theologians are treating the nation's violent racist past as if it were dead. But, as William Faulkner said, "the past is never dead; it is not even past." Racism is so deeply embedded in American history and culture that we cannot get rid of this cancer simply by ignoring it.

There can be no justice without memory—without remembering the horrible crimes committed against humanity and the great human struggles for justice. But oppressors always try to erase the history of their crimes and often portray themselves as the innocent ones. Through their control of the media and religious, political, and academic discourse "they're able," as Malcolm put it, "to make the victim look like the criminal and the criminal to look like the victim."[8]

Even when white theologians reflect on God and suffering, the problem of theodicy, they almost never make racism a central issue in their analysis of the challenge that evil poses for the Christian faith. If they should happen to mention racism, it is usually just a footnote or only a marginal comment. They almost never make racism the subject of a sustained analysis. It is amazing that racism could be so prevalent and violent in American life and yet so absent in white theological discourse.

President Clinton's call for a national dialogue on race has created a context for public debate in the churches, the academy, and the broader society. Where are the white theologians? What guidance are they providing for this debate? Are they creating a theological understanding of racism that enables whites to have a meaningful conversation with blacks and other people of color? Unfortunately, instead of searching for an understanding of the great racial divide, white religion scholars are doing their searching in the form of a third quest for the historical Jesus. I am not opposed to this academic quest. But if we could get a significant number of white theologians to study racism as seriously as they investigate the historical Jesus and other academic topics, they might discover how deep the cancer of racism is embedded not only in the society but also in the narrow way in which the discipline of theology is understood.

Although black liberation theology emerged out of the Civil Rights and Black Power movements of the 1960s, white theologians ignored it as if it were not worthy to be regarded as an academic discipline. It was not until Orbis Books published the translated works of Latin American liberation theologians that white North American male theologians cautiously began to talk and write about liberation theology and God's solidarity with the poor. But they still ignored the black poor in the United States, Africa, and Latin America. Our struggle to make sense out of the fight for racial justice was dismissed as too narrow and divisive. White U.S. theologians used the Latin American focus on class to minimize and even dismiss the black focus on race. African-Americans wondered how U.S. whites could take sides with the poor out there in Latin America without first siding with the poor here in North America. It was as if they had forgotten about their own complicity in the suffering of the black poor, who often were only a stone's throw from the seminaries and universities where they taught theology.

White theology's amnesia about racism is due partly to the failure of black theologians to mount a persistently radical race critique of Christian theology—one so incisive and enduring that no one could do theology without engaging white supremacy in the modern world. American and European theologians became concerned about anti-Semitism only because Jews did not let them forget the Christian complicity in the Holocaust. Feminists transformed the consciousness of American theologians through persistent, hard-hitting analysis of the evils of patriarchy, refusing to let any man anywhere in the world forget the past and present male assault against women. It is always the organic, or "grassroots," intellectuals of an exploited group, rather than the elite, who must take the lead in exposing the hidden crimes of criminals.

While black theologians' initial attack on white religion shocked white theologians, we did not shake the racist foundation of modern white theology.[9] With the assistance of James Forman's "Black Manifesto"[10] and the black caucuses in Protestant denominations, black theological critiques of racism were successful in shaking up the white churches. But white theologians in the seminaries, university departments of religion and divinity schools, and professional societies refused to acknowledge white supremacy as a theological problem and continued their business as usual, as if the lived experience of blacks was theologically vacuous.

One reason black theologians have not developed an enduring radical race critique stems from our uncritical identification with the dominant Christian and integrationist tradition in African-American history. We are the children of the Black Church and the Civil Rights movement. The spirituals have informed our theology more than the blues, Howard Thurman more than W. E. B. Du Bois, Martin Luther King, Jr., more than Malcolm X, and prominent male preachers more than radical women writers. We failed to sustain the critical side of the black theological dialectic and opted for acceptance into white Christian America. When whites opened the door to receive a token number of us into the academy, church, and society, the radical edge of our race critique was quickly dropped as we enjoyed our newfound privileges.

Womanist and second generation black male theologians, biblical scholars, and historians are moving in the right directions. The strength of these new intellectual developments lies in their refusal to simply repeat the ideas of the original advocates of black theology. They are breaking new theological ground, building on, challenging, and moving beyond the founders of black liberation theology. Using the writings of Zora Neale

Hurston, Alice Walker, Toni Morrison, and a host of other women writers past and present, womanist theologians broke the monopoly of black male theological discourse. They challenged the male advocates of black theology to broaden their narrow focus on race and liberation and incorporate gender, class, and sexuality critiques and the themes of survival and quality of life in our theological discourse.[11] Some younger black male critics locate the limits of black liberation theology in its focus on blackness,[12] and others urge a deeper commitment to it, focusing especially on the slave narratives.[13] Still others suggest that the Christian identity of black theology contributes to black passivity in the face of suffering.[14] Biblical scholars and historians are laying exegetical and historical foundations for a critical rereading of the Bible in the light of the history and culture of black people.[15] All these critiques and proposals make important contributions to the future development of black theology. What troubles me about all these new theological constructs, however, is the absence of a truly radical race critique.

Malcolm X was the most formidable race critic in the United States during the twentieth century. He was the great master of suspicion in regard to American democracy and the Christian faith. His critique of racism in Christianity and American culture was so forceful that even black Christians were greatly disturbed when they heard his analysis. His contention that "Christianity was a white man's religion" was so persuasive that many black Christians left churches to join the Nation of Islam. The rapid growth of the religion of Islam in the African-American community is largely due to the effectiveness of Malcolm's portrayal of Christianity as white nationalism. It was Malcolm via the Black Power movement who forced black theologians to take a critical look at white religion and to develop a hermeneutic of suspicion regarding black Christianity. How can African-Americans merge the "double self"—the black and the Christian—"into a better and truer self,"[16] especially since Africa is the object of ridicule in the modern world and Christianity is hardly distinguishable from European culture?

While we black theologians appropriated Malcolm in our initial critique of white religion, we did not wrestle with Malcolm long enough. We quickly turn to Martin King. The mistake was not in moving toward King but rather in leaving Malcolm behind. We need them both as a double-edged sword to slay the dragon of theological racism. Martin and Malcolm represent the yin and yang in the black attack on white supremacy. One without the other misses the target—the affirmation of blackness in the beloved community of humankind.

Malcolm alone makes it too easy for blacks to go it alone and for whites to say "begone!" Martin alone makes it easy for whites to ask for reconciliation without justice and for middle-class blacks to grant it, as long as they are treated specially. Putting Martin and Malcolm together enables us to overcome the limitations of each and to build on the strengths of both and thereby move blacks, whites, and other Americans (including Indians, Asians, Hispanics, gays, lesbians, and bisexuals) toward healing and understanding.

There can be no racial healing without dialogue, without ending the white silence on racism. There can be no reconciliation without honest and frank conversation. White supremacy is still with us in the academy, in the churches, and in every segment of the society because we would rather push this problem under the rug than find a way to deal with its past and present manifestations.

Most whites do not like to talk about white supremacy because it makes them feel guilty, a truly uncomfortable feeling. They would rather forget about the past and think only about the present and future. I understand that. I only ask whites to consider how uncomfortable the victims of white supremacy must feel, as they try to cope with the attitudes of whites who act as if white supremacy ceased with the passage of the 1964 Civil Rights Bill. At least when people express their racism overtly, there is some public recognition of its existence and a possibility of racial healing. Silence is racism's best friend.

"A time comes when silence is betrayal,"[17] Martin King said. That time has come for white theologians. White supremacy is one of the great contradictions of the gospel in modern times. White theologians who do not oppose racism publicly and rigorously engage it in their writings are a part of the problem and must be exposed as the enemy of justice. No one, therefore, can be neutral or silent in the face of this great evil. We are either for it or against it.

Black theologians must end their silence too. We have opposed racism much too gently. We have permitted white theological silence in exchange for the rewards of being accepted by the white theological establishment. This is a terrible price to pay for the few crumbs that drop from the white master's table. We must replace theological deference with courage, and thereby confront openly and lovingly silent white racists or be condemned as participants in the betrayal of our own people.

In 1903 W. E. B. Du Bois prophesied, "The problem of the twentieth century is the problem of the color-line,—the relation of the darker to the lighter races of [people] in Asia and Africa, in America and the islands of the sea."[18] As we stand at the threshold of the next century, that remarkable prophesy is as relevant today as it was when Du Bois uttered it. The challenge for black theology in the twenty-first century is to develop an enduring race critique that is so comprehensively woven into Christian understanding that no one will be able to forget the horrible crimes of white supremacy in the modern world.

Whose Earth Is It, Anyway?

The earth is the Lord's and all that is in it,
The world, and those who live in it.

—*Psalm 24:1 (RSV)*

We say the earth is our mother—we cannot own her; she owns us.

—*Pacific peoples*

The logic that led to slavery and segregation in the Americas, colonization and apartheid in Africa, and the rule of white supremacy throughout the world is the same one that leads to the exploitation of animals and the ravaging of nature. It is a mechanistic and instrumental logic that defines everything and everybody in terms of their contribution to the development and defense of white world supremacy. People who fight against white racism but fail to connect it to the degradation of the earth are anti-ecological—whether they know it or not. People who struggle against environmental degradation but do not incorporate in it a disciplined and sustained fight against white supremacy are racists—whether they acknowledge it or not. The fight for justice cannot be segregated but must be integrated with the fight for life in all its forms.

Until recently, the ecological crisis had not been a major theme in the liberation movements in the African-American community. "Blacks don't care about the environment" is a typical comment by white ecologists. Racial and economic justice has been at best only a marginal concern in the mainstream environmental movement. "White people care more about the endangered whale and the spotted owl than they do about the survival of young blacks in our nation's cities" is a well-founded belief in the African-American community. Justice fighters for blacks and the defenders of the earth have tended to ignore each other in their public discourse and practice. Their separation from each other is unfortunate because they are fighting the same enemy—human beings' domination of one another and nature.

The leaders in the mainstream environmental movement are mostly middle and upper-class whites who are unprepared culturally and intellectually to dialogue with angry blacks. The leaders in the African-American community are leery of talking about anything with whites that will distract from the menacing reality of racism. What both groups fail to realize is how much they need each other in the struggle for "justice, peace, and the integrity of creation."[1]

In this essay I want to challenge the black freedom movement to take a critical look at itself through the lens of the ecological movement and to challenge the ecological movement to critique itself through a radical and ongoing engagement of racism in American history and culture. I hope we can break the silence and promote genuine solidarity between the two groups and thereby enhance the quality of life for the whole inhabited earth—humankind and otherkind.

Expanding the Race Critique

Connecting racism with the degradation of the earth is a much-needed work in the African-American community, especially in black liberation theology and the black churches. Womanist theologians have already begun this important intellectual work. Delores Williams explores a "parallel between defilement of black women's bodies" and the exploitation of nature. Emilie Townes views "toxic waste landfills in African-American communities" as "contemporary versions of lynching a whole people." Karen Baker-Fletcher, using prose and poetry, appropriates the biblical and literary metaphors of dust and spirit to speak about the embodiment of God in creation. "Our task," she writes, "is to grow large hearts, large minds, reconnecting with earth, Spirit, and one another. Black religion must grow ever deeper in the heart."[2]

The leadership of African-American churches turned its much-needed attention toward ecological issues in the early 1990s. The catalyst, as usual in the African-American community, was a group of black churchwomen in Warren County, North Carolina, who in 1982 lay their bodies down on a road before dump trucks carrying soil contaminated with highly toxic PCBs (polychlorinated biphenyl) to block their progress. In two weeks more than four hundred protesters were arrested, "the first time anyone in the United States had been jailed trying to halt a toxic waste landfill."[3] Although local residents were not successful in stopping the landfill construction, that incident sparked the attention of Civil Rights and black church leaders and initiated the national environmental justice movement. In 1987 the United Church of Christ Commission of Racial Justice issued its groundbreaking "Report on Race and Toxic Wastes in the United States." This study found that "among a variety of indicators race was the best predictor of the location of hazardous waste facilities in the U.S."[4] Forty percent of the nation's commercial hazardous waste landfill capacity was in the three predominant African-American and Hispanic communities. The largest landfill in the nation is found in Sumter County, Alabama, where nearly 70 percent of its seventeen thousand residents are black and 96 percent are poor.

In October 1991 the First National People of Color Environmental Leadership Summit was convened in Washington, D.C. More than 650 grassroots and national leaders from fifty states, the District of Columbia, Mexico, Puerto Rico, and the Marshall Islands participated. They represented more than three hundred environmental groups of color. They all agreed that "[i]f this nation is to achieve environmental justice, the environment in urban ghettoes, barrios, reservations, and rural poverty pockets must be given the same protection as that provided to the suburbs."[5]

The knowledge that people of color are disproportionately affected by environmental pollution angered the black church community and fired up its leadership to take a more active role in fighting against "environmental racism," a phrase coined by Benjamin Chavis who was then the Director of the UCC Commission on Racial Justice.[6] Bunyan Bryant, a professor in the School of Natural Resources and Environment at the University of Michigan and a participant in the environmental justice movement, defines environmental racism as "an extension of racism":

> It refers to those institutional rules, regulations, and policies or government or corporate decisions that deliberately target certain communities for least desirable land uses, resulting in the disproportionate exposure of toxic and hazardous waste on communities based upon certain prescribed biological characteristics. Environmental racism is the unequal protection against toxic and hazardous waste exposure and the systematic exclusion of people of color from environmental decisions affecting their communities.[7]

The more blacks found out about the racist policies of the government and corporations the more determined they became in their opposition to environmental injustice. In December 1993, under the sponsorship of the National Council of Churches, leaders of mainline black churches held a historic two-day summit meeting on the environment in Washington, D.C. They linked environmental issues with civil rights and economic justice. They did not talk much about the ozone layer, global warming, the endangered whale, or the spotted owl. They focused primarily on the urgent concerns of their communities: toxic and hazardous wastes, lead poisoning, landfills and incinerators. "We have been living next to the train tracks, trash dumps, coal plants and insect-infested swamps for many decades," Bishop Frederick C. James of the A.M.E. Church said. "We in the black community have been disproportionately affected by toxic dumping, disproportionately affected by lead paint at home, disproportionately affected by dangerous chemicals in the workplace." Black clergy also linked local problems with global issues. "If toxic waste is not safe enough to be dumped in the United States, it is not safe enough to be dumped in Ghana, Liberia, Somalia nor anywhere else in the world," proclaimed Charles G. Adams, pastor of Hartford Memorial Baptist Church in Detroit. "If hazardous materials are not fit to be disposed of in the suburbs, they are certainly not fit to be disposed of in the cities."[8]

Like black church leaders, African-American politicians also are connecting social justice issues with ecology. According to the League of Conservation Voters, the Congressional Black Caucus has "the best environmental record of any voting bloc in Congress."[9] "Working for clean air, clean water, and a clean planet," declared Representative John Lewis of Georgia, "is just as important, if not more important, than anything I have ever worked on, including civil rights."[10]

Black and other poor people in all racial groups receive much less than their fair share of everything good in the world and a disproportionate amount of the bad. Middle-class and elite white environmentalists have been very effective in implementing the slogan "Not in My Backyard" (NIMBY). As a result, corporations and the government merely turned to the backyards of the poor to deposit their toxic waste. The poor live in the least desirable areas of our cities and rural communities. They work in the most polluted and physically dangerous workplaces. Decent health care hardly exists. With fewer resources to cope with the dire consequences of pollution, the poor bear an unequal burden for technological development while the rich reap most of the benefits. This makes racism and poverty ecological issues. If blacks and other hard-hit communities do not raise these ethical and political problems, they will continue to die a slow and silent death on the planet.

Every sphere of human existence is determined by ecology. It is not just an elitist or a white middle-class issue. A clean, safe environment is a human and civil rights issue that impacts the lives of poor blacks and other marginal groups. We therefore must not let the fear of distracting from racism blind us to the urgency of the ecological crisis. What good is it to eliminate racism if we are not around to enjoy a racist-free environment?

The survival of the earth, therefore, is a moral issue for everybody. If we do not save the earth from destructive human behavior, no one will survive. That fact alone ought to be enough to inspire people of all colors to join hands in the fight for a just and sustainable planet.

Expanding the Ecological Critique

We are indebted to ecologists in all fields and areas of human endeavor for sounding the alarm about the earth's distress. They have been so effective in raising ecological awareness that few people deny that our planet is in deep trouble. For the first time in history, humankind has the knowledge and power to destroy all life—either with a nuclear bang or a gradual poisoning of the land, air, and sea.

Scientists have warned us of the dire consequences of what human beings are doing to the environment. Theologians and ethicists have raised the moral and religious issues. Grassroots activists in many communities are organizing to stop the killing of nature and its creatures. Politicians are paying attention to people's concern for a clean, safe environment. "It is not so much a question of whether the lion will one day lie down with the lamb," writes Alice Walker, "but whether human beings will ever be able to lie down with any creature or being at all."[11]

What is absent from much of the talk about the environment in First World countries is a truly radical critique of the culture most responsible for the ecological crisis. This is especially true among white ethicists and theologians in the United States. In most of the essays and books I have read, there is hardly a hint that perhaps whites could learn something of how we got into this ecological mess from those who have been the victims of white world supremacy. White ethicists and theologians sometimes refer to the disproportionate impact of hazardous waste on blacks and other people of color in the United States and Third World, and even cite an author or two, here and there throughout the development of their discourse on ecology. They often include a token black or Indian in anthologies on ecotheology, ecojustice, and ecofeminism. It is "politically correct" to demonstrate a knowledge of and concern for people of color in progressive theological circles. But people of color are not treated *seriously*, that is, as if they have something *essential* to contribute to the conversation. Environmental justice concerns of poor people of color hardly ever merit serious attention, not to mention organized resistance. How can we create a genuinely mutual ecological dialogue between whites and people of color if one party acts as if they have all the power and knowledge?

Since Earth Day in 1970, the environmental movement has grown into a formidable force in American society, and ecological reflections on the earth have become a dominant voice in religion, influencing all disciplines. It is important to ask, however, whose problems define the priorities of the environmental movement? Whose suffering claims its attention? "Do environmentalists care about poor people?"[12] Environmentalists usually respond something like Rafe Pomerance puts it: "A substantial element of our agenda has related to improving the environment for everybody."[13] Others tell a different story. Former Assistant Secretary of Interior James Joseph says that "environmentalists tend to focus on those issues that provide recreative outlets instead of issues that focus on equity." Black activist Cliff Boxley speaks even more bluntly, labeling the priorities of environmentalists as "green bigotry." "Conservationists are more interested in saving the habitats of birds than in the construction of low-income housing."[14]

Do we have any reason to believe that the culture most responsible for the ecological crisis will also provide the moral and intellectual resources for the earth's liberation? White ethicists and theologians apparently think so, since so much of their discourse about theology and the earth is just talk among themselves. But I have a deep suspicion about the theological and ethical values of white culture and religion. For five centuries whites have acted as if they owned the world's resources and have forced people of color to accept their scientific and ethical values. People of color have studied dominant theologies and ethics because our physical and spiritual survival partly depended on it. Now that humanity has reached the possibility of extinction, one would think that a critical assessment of how we got to where we are would be the next step for sensitive and caring theologians of the earth. While there is some radical questioning along these lines, it has not been persistent or challenging enough to compel whites to look outside of their dominating culture for ethical and cultural resources for the earth's salvation. One can still earn a doctorate degree in ethics and theology at American seminaries, even here at Union Seminary in New York, and not seriously engage racism in this society and the world. If we save the planet and have a society of inequality, we wouldn't have saved much.

According to Audre Lorde, "the master's tools will never dismantle the master's house."[15] They are too narrow and thus assume that people of color have nothing to say about race, gender, sexuality, and the earth—all of which are interconnected. We need theologians and ethicists who are interested in mutual dialogue, honest conversation about justice for the earth and all of its inhabitants. We need whites who are eager to know something about the communities of people of color—our values, hopes, and dreams. Whites know so little about our churches and communities that it is often too frustrating to even talk to them about anything that matters. Dialogue requires respect and knowledge of the other—their history, culture, and religion. No one racial or national group has all the answers, but all groups have something to contribute to the earth's healing.

Many ecologists speak often of the need for humility and mutual dialogue. They tell us that we are all interrelated and interdependent, including human- and otherkind. The earth is not a machine. It is an organism in which all things are a part of one another. "Every entity in the universe," writes Catherine Keller, "can be described as a process of interconnection with every other being."[16] If white ecologists really believe that, why do most still live in segregated communities? Why are their essays and books about the endangered earth so monological—that is, a conversation of a dominant group talking to itself? Why is there so much talk of love, humility, interrelatedness, and interdependence, and yet so little of these values reflected in white people's dealings with people of color?

Blacks and other minorities are often asked why they are not involved in the mainstream ecological movement. To white theologians and ethicists I ask, "Why are you not involved in the dialogue on race?" I am not referring primarily to President Clinton's failed initiative, but to the initiative started by the Civil Rights and Black Power movements and black liberation theology more than forty years ago. How do we account for the conspicuous white silence on racism, not only in the society and world but especially in theology, ethics, and ecology? I have yet to read a white theologian or ethicist who has incorporated a sustained, radical critique of white supremacy in his/her theological discourse similar to the engagement of anti-Semitism, class contradictions, and patriarchy.

To be sure, a few concerned white theologians have written about their opposition to white racism but not because race critique was essential to their theological identity. It is usually just a gesture of support for people of color when solidarity across differences is in vogue. As soon as it is no longer socially and intellectually acceptable to talk about race, white theologians revert back to their silence. But as Elie Wiesel said in his Nobel Peace Prize Acceptance Speech, "we must always take sides. Neutrality helps the oppressor, never the victim. Silence encourages the tormentor, never the tormented."[17] Only when white theologians realize that a fight against racism is a fight for *their* humanity will we be able to create a coalition of blacks, whites, and other people of color in the struggle to save the earth.

Today ecology is in vogue and many people are talking about our endangered planet. I want to urge us to deepen our conversation by linking the earth's crisis with the crisis in the human family. If it is important to save the habitats of birds and other species, then it is at least equally important to save black lives in the ghettos and prisons of America. As Gandhi said, "the earth is sufficient for everyone's need but not for everyone's greed."[18]

Notes

Introduction: Looking Back, Going Forward

1. James Baldwin, *The Fire Next Time* (New York: Dell, 1964), p. 61.

2. Ibid., p. 21.

3. Ibid., p. 14.

4. Cited in Manning Marable, "The Black Faith of W. E. B. Du Bois: Sociocultural and Political Dimensions of Black Religion," *The Southern Quarterly* 23 (spring 1985), p. 21.

5. Theologian Langdon Gilkey of the University of Chicago made that observation to me in a private conversation. It is unfortunate that he never made a disciplined argument about King's theological importance in his published writings. If he had done so, perhaps American white theologians would not have been as hostile as they were to the rise of black liberation theology.

6. *Malcolm X Speaks*, ed. George Breitman (New York: Grove Press, 1965), pp. 107–108.

7. See *Washington Post*, 23 January 1994, p. G6.

8. *The Fire Next Time*, p. 46.

9. Many people called Malcolm X "the angriest Negro in America." See his *Autobiography* (New York: Ballantine Books, 1986), p. 366.

10. Audrey Smedley, *Race in North America: Origin and Evolution of a Worldview* (Boulder, Colo.: Westview Press, 1993), p. 117.

11. See Reinhold Niebuhr, *Moral Man and Immoral Society* (New York: Charles Scribner's Sons, 1932).

Section I: Black Theology and Black Power
Christianity and Black Power

1. Albert Camus, *The Rebel* (New York: Random House, 1956), p. 13.

2. Stokely Carmichael and Charles Hamilton, *Black Power: The Politics of Liberation in America* (New York: Random House, 1967), p. 47.

3. Friedrich Schleiermacher, *The Christian Faith*, trans. J. Baillie, 1922, p. 9.

Black Spirituals: A Theological Interpretation

1. W. E. B. Du Bois, *The Gift of Black Folk* (1924; reprint, New York: Washington Square Press, 1970), p. 158.

2. Cited in Vincent Harding, "Religion and Resistance Among Antebellum Negroes, 1800–1860," in *The Making of Black America*, vol. 1, ed. August Meier and Elliot Rudwick (New York: Atheneum, 1969), p. 181.

3. Comment by Guy Johnson of the University of North Carolina, cited in Sterling Stuckey, "Through the Prism of Folklore," in *Black and White in American Culture*, ed. J. Chametyky and S. Kaplan (Amherst: University of Massachusetts Press, 1969), p. 172.

4. Karl Marx and Friedrich Engels, *On Religion* (New York: Schocken Books, 1964), p. 42.

5. Miles Fisher, *Negro Slaves Songs in the United States* (New York: Citadel Press, 1953), pp. 27–28, 66–67, 181–185.

6. Ibid., p. 108. It is important to note that Fisher is quoting the conservative estimate of a southern historian.

7. See ibid., chapter 4. Fisher notes that the spirituals were used to convene secret meetings among slaves, and the colony of Virginia prohibited them as early as 1676 (pp. 29, 66ff.). Most colonies joined Virginia in outlawing the secret meetings, but "neither outlawry nor soldiery prevented [them] from hemispheric significance" (p. 67).

8. B. A. Botkin, ed. *Lay My Burden Down* (Chicago: University of Chicago Press, 1945), p. 26.

9. See *Negro Slave Songs*, chapters 1–4.

10. *Life and Times of Frederick Douglass* (1892; reprint, New York: Collier Books, 1962), p. 159.

Black Theology on Revolution, Violence, and Reconciliation

1. Jürgen Moltmann, *Religion, Revolution and the Future*, trans. Douglas Meeks (New York: Charles Scribner's Sons, 1969), p. 131.

2. "Man as Possibility," in *Cross Currents* 18 (summer 1968), p. 274.

3. *Religion, Revolution and the Future*, p. 132.

4. Ernst Bloch, *The City of God*, trans. Marcus Dods (New York: Modern Library, 1950), p. 694.

5. Cited in Roger Garaudy, *From Anathema to Dialogue* (New York: Vintage Books, 1968), p. 98.

6. Cited in Roland Bainton, *Here I Stand* (New York: Abingdon Press, 1950), p. 280.

7. Cited in *From Anathema to Dialogue*, p. 98.

8. George Celestin's "A Christian Looks at Revolution," in *New Theology No. 6*, ed. Martin Marty and Dean Peerman (London: Collier Macmillan, 1969), p. 69.

9. Jacques Ellul, *Violence*, trans. C. G. King's (New York: Seabury Press, 1969), p. 3. In this quotation, Ellul is not defending this viewpoint; he is explicating it.

10. For an account of this dialogue, see Thomas Ogletree, ed., *Opening for Marxist-Christian Dialogue* (Nashville: Abingdon Press, 1968).

11. See particularly Lehmann's *Ethics in a Christian Context* (New York: Harpers, 1963) and his *Ideology and Incarnation* (Geneva: John Knox Association, 1962).

12. *Religion, Revolution and the Future*, p. 103.

13. Ibid., pp. 104–105.

14. Vitaly Baroxoj, "Why the Gospels Are Revolutionary: The Foundation of a Theology in the Service of Social Revolutions," in IDO-C, ed., *When All Else Fails* (Philadelphia: Pilgrim Press, 1970).

15. Fred Hampton was the head of the Chicago branch of the Black Panther Party. He was killed December 4, 1969, in a police raid while sleeping in bed.

16. Thomas Merton, *Faith and Violence* (Notre Dame, Ind.: Notre Dame University Press, 1968), p. 3.

17. *Religion, Revolution and the Future*, p. 143.

18. Franz Fanon, *The Wretched of the Earth* (New York: Grove Press, 1965), p. 255.

19. Ernst Käsemann, *Jesus Means Freedom*, trans. Frank Clarke (London: SCM Press, 1969).

Black Theology and the Black Church: Where Do We Go from Here?

1. This statement first appeared in the *New York Times*, July 31, 1966, and is reprinted in Warner Traynham's *Christian Faith in Black and White* (Wakefield, Mass.: Parameter, 1973).

2. For an account of the rise of the concept of Black Power in the Civil Rights movement, see Stokely Carmichael and Charles Hamilton, *Black Power: The Politics of Black Liberation* (New York: Random House). For Martin King's viewpoint, see his *Where Do We Go from Here: Chaos or Community?* (Boston: Beacon Press, 1968).

3. Cited in Lawrence W. Levine, *Black Culture and Black Consciousness* (New York: Oxford University Press, 1977), p. 207.

4. This is especially true of Charles Long, who has been a provocative discussant about black theology. Unfortunately, he has not written much about this viewpoint. The only article I know on this subject is his "Perspectives for a Study of Afro-American Religion in the United States" (*History of Religions* 11, no. 1, August 1971).

5. The representatives of this perspective include Gayraud S. Wilmore, *Black Religion and Black Radicalism* (New York: Doubleday, 1972), and my brother, Cecil W. Cone, *Identity Crisis in Black Theology* (Nashville, Tenn.: A.M.E. Church, 1976).

6. This statement, issued on June 13, 1969, is also reprinted in *Christian Faith in Black and White* by Warner Traynham.

7. See Julius Nyerere, *Ujamaa: Essays on Socialism* (Dar es salaam: Oxford University Press, 1968), especially chapter 2, entitled "The Arusha Declaration," pp. 13–37.

8. Cited in Jose Miguez Bonino, *Christians and Marxists* (Grand Rapids, Mich.: Eerdmans, 1976), p. 76.

9. Cited in George Padmore, *Pan-Africanism or Communism* (New York: Anchor Books, 1972), p. 323.

10. Cited in *Christians and Marxists*, p. 71.

11. A quotation from Giulio Girardi, cited in *Christians and Marxists*, p. 71.

Section II: Martin and Malcolm

The Theology of Martin Luther King, Jr.

1. Martin Luther King, Jr., "Thou Fool," August 27, 1967, an unpublished sermon delivered at Mount Pisgah Baptist Church, Chicago, Illinois, p. 11. Martin Luther King, Jr., Papers, Series III, Martin Luther King, Jr., Center for Nonviolent Social Change, Atlanta, Georgia (hereafter referred to as King Center Archives).

2. In King's two versions of his "Pilgrimage to Nonviolence," the black religious tradition is not mentioned as an important contribution to his theological perspective. See his *Stride Toward Freedom* (New York: Harper, 1958), pp. 90–107 and

Strength to Love (1963; reprint, Philadelphia: Fortress, 1982), pp. 147–155. On the basis of these accounts alone, one could easily conclude that King did not recognize any important contribution of black religion on his theology. Perhaps he did not during the early years of his ministry but did so in the later years, as I will seek to demonstrate in this essay.

3. *Stride Toward Freedom*, p. 101.

4. King, Jr., *Who Speaks for the Negro?* (New York: Random House, 1965), p. 213.

5. Speaking of his "intellectual quest for a method to eliminate social evil," King said, "I came early to Walter Rauschenbusch's *Christianity and the Social Crisis*, which left an indelible imprint on my thinking by giving me a theological basis for the social concern which had already grown up in me as a result of my early experiences" (*Stride Toward Freedom*, p. 91). See especially chapters 1 and 2 of Rauschenbusch's *Christianity and the Social Crisis* (New York: Macmillan, 1907). For a detailed interpretation of Rauschenbusch's impact on King, see Kenneth L. Smith and Ira G. Zepp, Jr., *Search for the Beloved Community*, chapter 2; and of Ira G. Zepp, Jr., "Intellectual Sources of the Ethical Thought of Martin Luther King, Jr.," chapter 2 (hereafter referred to as "Intellectual Sources").

King's sense of social responsibility appeared early in his thinking. Referring to his call to the ministry on his Crozer application, he wrote: "My call to the ministry was quite different from most explanations I've heard. This decision came about the summer of 1944 when I felt an inescapable urge to serve society. In short, I felt a sense of responsibility which I could not escape."

6. Ibid., p. 100. For several treatments of the impact of personalism on King, see *Search for the Beloved Community*, chapter 5; "Intellectual Sources," chapter 5; L. Harold DeWolf, "Martin Luther King, Jr., as Theologian"; John Ansbro, *Making of a Mind: Martin Luther King, Jr.*, Chapter 3.

7. See ibid., p. 99. King wrote a paper on "Karl Barth's Conception of God" during his doctoral studies at Boston. His comments are typical of many American critics who have not understood Barth or who deliberately distort his theological perspective. Barth was neither an anti-rationalist nor a semi-fundamentalist. For a perspective on Barth similar to King's, see his teacher, L. Harold DeWolf, *The Religious Revolt Against Reason* (New York: Harper, 1949).

8. See especially *Stride Toward Freedom*, pp. 97–98. During his graduate education, King wrote several papers on Niebuhr. See "Reinhold Niebuhr" (14pp.) and "Reinhold Niebuhr's Ethical Dualism" (11pp.), King Center Archives. For a discussion of Niebuhr's influence, see *Search for the Beloved Community*, chapter 4; and "Intellectual Sources," chapter 4.

9. For Gandhi's influence upon King, see his "Sermon on Gandhi," March 22, 1959, Dexter Avenue Baptist Church, Montgomery, Alabama, King Center Archives. Also "My Trip to the Land of Gandhi," *Ebony*, July 1959. See also "Intellectual Sources," chapter 3.

10. *Stride Toward Freedom*, p. 179.

11. Ibid., p. 217.

12. According to black psychologist Clark, "King's insistence that the Negro cannot afford to be corroded by hatred and must therefore discipline himself to love those who despise him is consistent with the Christian tradition and is the antithesis of the doctrine preached by the Nationalists. On the surface, King's philosophy appears to reflect health and stability, while the Black Nationalists betray pathology and instability. A deeper analysis, however, might reveal an unrealistic, if not pathological basis in King's doctrine as well. It is questionable whether masses of an oppressed group can in fact 'love' their oppressor. The natural reactions to injustice, oppression, and humiliation are bitterness and resentment. . . . It would appear, then, that any demand that a victim love his oppressor—in contrast with a mere tactical application of nonviolent, dignified resistance as a moral rebuke with concomitant power to arouse the conscience and effectiveness of others—imposes an additional and probably intolerable psychological burden" (Kenneth Clark, *Dark Ghetto: The Dilemmas of Social Power* [New York: Harper Torchbooks, 1967], p. 218).

13. Henry David Thoreau, *Civil Disobedience* (Westwood, N.J.: Fleming Revel, 1964), p. 14.

14. Martin Luther King, Jr., "The Un-Christian Christian," *Ebony*, August 1965, p. 77.

15. See his often preached sermon, "A Knock at Midnight," June 25, 1967, King Center Archives.

16. Unless indicated otherwise, my account is taken from his sermon "Thou Fool," August 27, 1967, King Center Archives. See also *Stride Toward Freedom*, pp. 134–135; *Strength to Love*, pp. 113f.

17. *Stride for Freedom*, p. 135.

18. Speaking at the sixty-eighth annual convention of the Rabbinical Assembly, King said: "What is necessary now is to see integration in political terms where there is sharing of power. When we see integration in political terms, then we recognize that there are times when we must see segregation as a temporary way-

station to a truly integrated society." "Conversation with Martin Luther King," *Conservative Judaism*, 22 (spring 1968), p. 8.

19. There is no evidence that King moved away from his deep commitment to nonviolence. But he did recognize that the riots in the cities revealed that nonviolence must be taken to a new level of militancy which involved massive disruption of the operation of government. There are many references in King's writings to this change in his thinking during 1966–68. In *The Trumpet of Conscience* (New York: Harper, 1967), he said: "Nonviolent protest must now mature to a new level to correspond to heightened black impatience and stiffened white resistance. This new level is mass civil disobedience" (p. 15). See also "Showdown for Nonviolence," *Look*, 16 April 1968. For an important interpretation of this shift in King's thinking, see David Garrow, *Martin Luther King: Challenging America at Its Core* (New York: Democratic Socialists of America, 1983); and his *The FBI and Martin Luther King, Jr.* (New York: Norton, 1981), chapter 6.

20. The best sources for King's positive affirmations of black power and pride are his unpublished speeches on the "Pre-Washington Campaign," recruiting persons for the Poor People's March on Washington. In Clarksdale, Mississippi (March 19, 1968), he said: "We're going to let our children know that the only philosophers that lived were not Plato and Aristotle, but W. E. B. Du Bois and Alain Locke came through the universe" ("Address to Mass Meeting," p. 7, King Center Archives).

21. As early as 1965, King had become greatly disappointed with many white Christians and other moderates. "The white church . . . has greatly disappointed me. . . . As the Negro struggles against grave injustice, most white churchmen offer pious irrelevancies and sanctimonious trivialities. . . . Over the past several years, I must say, I have been gravely disappointed with white 'moderates.' I am often inclined to think that they are more of a stumbling block to the Negro's progress than the White Citizen's Counciler or the Ku Klux Klanner" (*Playboy*, January 1965). King's classic critique of the white church and other moderates is found in his "Letter from Birmingham Jail" in his *Why We Can't Wait* (New York: Harper, 1963).

22. There are many references of King concerning his dream being turned into a nightmare. One of his most extended statements in this regard is found in *The Trumpet of Conscience*, pp. 75–76.

23. See "Beyond Vietnam: Dr. Martin Luther King's Prophecy for the '80s," a pamphlet of the Clergy and Laity Concerned, p. 2.

24. *Stride Toward Freedom*, pp. 59–60.

25. Martin Luther King, Jr., "Address to the Initial Mass Meeting of the Montgomery Improvement Association," Holt Street Baptist Church, December 5, 1955 (King Center Archives), hereafter referred to as "Holt Street Address."

26. See *Stride Toward Freedom*, p. 62.

27. "Holt Street Address."

28. Ibid. In *Stride Toward Freedom*, King reported: "I urged the people not to force anybody to refrain from riding the buses. 'Our method will be that of persuasion, not coercion.' Emphasizing the Christian doctrine of love, '[O]ur actions must be guided by the deepest principles of our Christian faith. Love must be our regulating ideal. Once again we must hear the words of Jesus echoing across the centuries: 'Love your enemies, bless them that curse you and pray for them that despitefully use you.' In spite of the mistreatment that we have confronted we must not become bitter, and end up by hating our white brothers. As Booker T. Washington said, 'Let no man pull you so low as to make you hate him' " (p. 62). There is nothing like this statement in the original address. There is no reference to Booker T. Washington.

29. Although much research is needed in order to determine the "essential writings" of Martin King, any student of King who has examined the materials at the King Center Archives can easily observe that many of his speeches and much of the material for his books were ghost-written. Working for the movement twenty hours a day, traveling 325 thousand miles and making 450 speeches a year, it was not possible for King to write everything that was published under his name.

30. *Stride Toward Freedom*, p. 84.

31. See Bayard Rustin, "Montgomery Diary," in his *Down the Line* (Chicago: Quadrangle Books, 1971), pp. 55–61. Originally published in *Liberation*, April 1956. See also G. Smiley, "An Interview with Martin Luther King, Jr.," February–March 1956, King Center Archives.

32. See his thirty-page speech at the staff retreat, November 14, 1966, Frogmore, S.C., p. 14. Also important is his address to the 10th Convention of SCLC, August 16, 1967, King Center Archives. Several of King's associates have confirmed his openness to socialism. See David Garrow's interpretation of his socialist leanings in "From Reformer to Revolutionary" and "The Radical Challenge of Martin King," *FBI and Martin Luther King, Jr.*, chapter 6. In a February 27, 1985, letter to David Garrow, C. L. R. James says he remembered that Martin King articulated "ideas which were fundamentally Marxist-Leninist." According to James's recollection, King said: "I don't say such things from the pulpit, James, but that is what I really believe." For a guarded assessment, see also Adam Fairclough, "Was Martin

Luther King a Marxist?" in *History Workshop*, a journal of socialist and feminist historians, spring 1983, pp. 117–125.

33. Martin Luther King, Jr., "In Search for a Sense of Direction," February 7, 1968, fourteen-page address, Vermont Avenue Baptist Church, Washington, D.C., pp. 1, 2, King Center Archives.

34. This statement appears in many of King's addresses and sermons. See especially "Address to Ministers' Leadership Training Program," "Pre-Washington Campaign—to Minister to the Valley," February 23, 1968, p. 18, King Center Archives.

35. Martin Luther King, Jr., "But If Not . . . ," November 5, 1967, Ebenezer Baptist Church, Atlanta, King Center Archives.

36. "Standing by the Best in an Evil Time," August 6, 1967, Ebenezer Baptist Church, Atlanta, King Center Archives. For two good discussions of the development of King's views on Vietnam, see Russell E. Dowdy, "Nonviolence vs. Nonexistence: The Vietnam War and Martin Luther King, Jr." M.A. thesis in the Dept. of History, North Carolina State University, 1983; Adam Fairclough, "Martin Luther King, Jr., and the War in Vietnam," *Phylon*, 45, no. 1 (1984), pp. 19–39. See also Fairclough's excellent "Study of the Southern Christian Leadership Conference and the Rise and Fall of the Nonviolent Civil Rights Movement," Ph.D. diss., University of Keele, U.K., 1977.

Martin Luther King, Jr., Black Theology—Black Church

1. Alex Haley, "Playboy Interview with Martin Luther King," *Playboy* 12 (January 1965), pp. 70–71.

2. Ibid., p. 66.

3. For an interpretation of nationalism and integration in the history of black religious thought, see Gayraud S. Wilmore, *Black Religion and Black Radicalism*, 2d ed. (Maryknoll, N.Y.: Orbis Books, 1983); see also Francis L. Broderick, "The Gnawing Dilemma: Separatism and Integration, 1865–1925," in *Key Issues in the Afro-American Experience*, vol. 2, Nathan Huggins, Martin Kilson, and Daniel Fox (New York: Harcourt Brace Jovanovich, 1971).

Martin Luther King, Jr., and the Third World

1. Today black South Africans and their supporters, under the leadership of Archbishop Desmond Tutu, Allan Boesak, Nelson Mandela, and Winnie Mandela,

and a host of others in the African National Congress and similar organizations, are currently engaged in a protracted life-and-death struggle against apartheid.

2. Cited in Coretta Scott King, *My Life with Martin Luther King, Jr.* (New York: Holt, Rinehart and Winston, 1969), p. 294.

3. In this essay I limit my analysis chiefly to two periods in Martin Luther King, Jr.'s thinking. However, I have found three periods in the development of his life and thought from the time of the Montgomery bus boycott (Dec. 5, 1955) to his assassination (April 4, 1968). The first period is quite brief (early weeks of the boycott) and is defined by his primary focus on *justice*. The second period (early 1956 to fall 1965) focuses primarily on *love*; the third period (1966 to his assassination in 1968) focuses primarily on *hope*. The distinctions are not rigid but rather a matter of emphases in his thinking. In all periods the concerns for justice, love, and hope are present and intertwined. For an interpretation of the development of King's thinking in terms of the three periods, see James H. Cone, "The Theology of Martin Luther King, Jr.," *Union Seminary Quarterly Review*, 40, no. 4 (1986), pp. 21–39.

4. See Martin Luther King, Jr., "The Legitimacy of the Struggle in Montgomery," statement, May 4, 1956, Martin Luther King, Jr., Papers (Martin Luther King, Jr., Center for Nonviolent Social Change, Atlanta), hereafter referred to as King Papers. Martin Luther King, Jr., "The Birth of a New Age," August 7–11, 1956, p. 86, ibid.

5. "Birth of a New Age." King also used this statement in his first major address, and it was repeated in several others. See "Address at Holt Street Baptist Church," December 5, 1955, King Papers.

6. Martin Luther King, Jr., "Facing the Challenge of a New Age," *Phylon* 18 (April 1957), p. 26. This is essentially the address delivered at the Alpha Phi Alpha convention in August 1956, "Birth of a New Age." See Martin Luther King, Jr., "The Time for Freedom Has Come," *New York Times Magazine*, September 10, 1961, pp. 25, 118–119, 25. The quotation from Victor Hugo was frequently used in King's addresses.

7. For King's interpretation of the impact the independence celebration of Ghana had on him, see especially Martin Luther King, Jr., "Birth of a New Nation," address, Dexter Avenue Baptist Church, April 1957, King Papers. See also Homer Jack, "Conversation in Ghana," *Christian Century*, April 10, 1957, pp. 446–448. For King's interpretation of his trip to India, see Martin Luther King, Jr., "My Trip

to the Land of Gandhi," *Ebony* 14 (July 1959), pp. 84–92; Martin Luther King, Jr., "Sermon on Gandhi," March 22, 1959, King Papers. See also Swami Vishwananda, *With the Kings in India* (New Delhi, 1959); Martin Luther King, Jr., "Farewell Statement," New Delhi, India, March 9, 1959, King Papers; and "Statement of Dr. King upon Landing at New York City," March 18, 1959, ibid.

8. "Letter from Birmingham City Jail," *New Leader*, June 24, 1963, p. 8.

9. *Strength to Love* (Philadelphia: Fortress Press, 1981), p. 154; *Stride Toward Freedom* (New York: Harper, 1958), p. 44.

10. See "The American Dream," *Negro History Bulletin* 31 (May 1968), pp. 10–15. The essay was a commencement address at Lincoln University, June 6, 1961.

11. Ibid.

12. "The Acceptance Speech of Martin Luther King, Jr. of the Nobel Peace Prize on December 10, 1964," *Negro History Bulletin* 31 (May 1968), p. 21. See "The Quest for Peace and Justice," Nobel Lecture, Oslo, Norway, December 11, 1964, pp. 1, 5, King Papers.

13. "Playboy Interview: Martin Luther King," a reprint from *Playboy* 12 (January 1965).

14. "Transforming a Neighborhood into a Brotherhood," address for the National Association of Real Estate Brokers, August 10, 1967, p. 9, King Papers.

15. See "Next Stop: The North," *Saturday Review*, 13 November 1965, pp. 33–35, 105. For his response to Watts, see *Where Do We Go from Here: Chaos or Community?* (Boston: Beacon Press, 1968), p. 112.

16. James Bevel, one of King's aides, spoke often of the Chicago slums as a "system of internal colonialism." King also adopted the same description. See his "Chicago Plan," January 7, 1966, p. 3, King Papers. "European Tour," speech, March 1966, p. 8, ibid.

17. *Where Do We Go from Here?*, p. 133.

18. Ibid.

19. See "Thou Fool," sermon, Mt. Pisgah Missionary Baptist Church, Chicago, August 27, 1967, p. 14, King Papers. This sermon includes King's account of the deep crisis of fear during the Montgomery bus boycott that led to his appropriation of the faith of his early childhood. I think this is the most critical turning point in King's life. Although I have always maintained that King's faith, as defined by the Black Church, was indispensable for understanding his life and thought, David J. Garrow was the first person to identify King's "kitchen experience" (as it might be

called) as the decisive experience in defining his faith. See David J. Garrow, "Martin Luther King, Jr., and the Spirit of Leadership," *Journal of American History* 74 (September 1987), pp. 438–438, and *Bearing the Cross: Martin Luther King, Jr., and the Southern Christian Leadership Conference, 1955–1968* (New York: W. Morrow, 1986); and Cone, "Theology of King," pp. 26–39.

20. Luke 1:52 RSV.

21. See Adam Fairclough, "Martin Luther King, Jr., and the War in Vietnam," *Phylon* 45, no. 1 (1984), pp. 19–39. See also Russell E. Dowdy, "Nonviolence vs. Nonexistence: The Vietnam War and Martin Luther King, Jr.," M.A. thesis, North Carolina State University, 1983. On King's dream being turned into a nightmare, see his *The Trumpet of Conscience* (New York: Harper and Row, 1968), pp. 75f.

22. "Why I Am Opposed to the War in Vietnam," sermon, April 30, 1967, p. 8, King Papers.

23. "A Testament of Hope," a reprint from *Playboy* 16 (January 1969), p. 4; "Why I Am Opposed," p. 6.

24. "Why I Am Opposed," pp. 3, 4.

25. "Standing by the Best in an Evil Time," sermon, August 6, 1967, pp. 7–8, King Papers.

26. *Martin Luther King, Jr.: Beyond Vietnam, April 4, 1967, Riverside Church* (New York, 1982), p. 1, pamphlet, King Papers; "Speech at Staff Retreat," May 29–31, 1967, ibid.; and address at a rally of the Pre-Washington Campaign, March 22, 1968, p. 7, ibid.

27. *Trumpet of Conscience*, p. 76.

28. "The Other America," address, March 10, 1968, p. 11, King Papers.

29. "Facing the Challenge of a New Age," p. 34.

30. Ibid.

31. Cited in Pat Watters, *Down to Now: Reflections on the Southern Civil Rights Movement* (New York: Pantheon Books, 1971), p. 366.

32. "To Minister to the Valley," address, February 23, 1968, p. 21, King Papers.

Section III: Going Forward

New Roles in the Ministry: A Theological Appraisal

1. "Double Jeopardy: To Be Black and Female," in *Black Woman*, ed. Toni Cade (New York: Signet Books, 1970), p. 92.

2. Cited by Renée Ferguson, "Women's Liberation Has a Different Meaning for Blacks," in Gerda Lerner, *Black Women in White America: A Documentary History* (New York: Random House, 1973), p. 588.

White Theology Revisited

1. See William Julius Wilson, *The Truly Disadvantaged: The Inner City, the Underclass and Public Policy* (Chicago: University of Chicago Press, 1987).

2. Basil Davidson, *The African Slave Trade: Precolonial History, 1450–1850* (Boston: Little, Brown, 1961), p. 80.

3. Eduardo Galeano, *Open Veins of Latin America: Five Centuries of the Pillage of a Continent* (London: Monthly Review Press, 1973), p. 50.

4. See Adam Hochschild, "Hearts of Darkness: Adventures in the Slave Trade," *San Francisco Examiner Magazine*, August 16, 1998, p. 13. This essay is an excerpt from his book, *King Leopold's Ghosts: A Story of Greed, Terror, and Heroism in Colonial Africa* (New York: Houghton Mifflin, 1998). Louis Turner suggests that 5 to 8 million were killed in the Congo. See his *Multinational Companies and the Third World* (New York: Hill and Wang, 1973), p. 27.

5. See especially Winthrop D. Jordan, *White over Black: American Attitudes Toward the Negro, 1550–1812* (Baltimore: Penguin Books, 1969).

6. Cited in Martin E. Marty, *Righteous Empire: The Protestant Experience in America* (New York: Dial Press, 1970), p. 17.

7. See Reinhold Niebuhr, "Man's Tribalism as One Source of His Inhumanity," in *Man's Nature and His Communities* (New York: Charles Scribner's Sons, 1965), pp. 84–105; and his "Justice to the American Negro from State, Community, and Church," in *Pious and Secular America* (New York: Charles Scribner's Sons, 1958), pp. 78–85.

8. *Malcolm X Speaks* (New York: Grove Press, 1965), p. 165.

9. In addition to *Black Theology and Black Power*, my contribution to black theology's race critique included *A Black Theology of Liberation* (1970; reprint, Maryknoll, N.Y.: Orbis Books, 1985) and *God of the Oppressed* (1975; reprint, Maryknoll, N.Y.: Orbis Books, 1998). Other critiques were Albert B. Cleage, *The Black Messiah* (New York: Sheed and Ward, 1968); J. Deotis Roberts, *Liberation and Reconciliation: A Black Theology* (1971; reprint, Maryknoll, N.Y.: Orbis Books, 1994) and *A Black Political Theology* (Philadelphia: Westminster Press/John Knox Press, 1974); and Gayraud S. Wilmore's *Black Religion and Black Radicalism* (1972; reprint, Mary-

knoll, N.Y.: Orbis Books, 1998). Significant essays included Vincent Harding, "Black Power and the American Christ," *Christian Century* (January 4, 1967), and "The Religion of Black Power," in *Religious Situation, 1968*, ed. D. R. Cutler (Boston: Beacon Press, 1968); and Herbert O. Edwards, "Racism and Christian Ethics in America," *Katallagete* (winter 1971).

10. See "The Black Manifesto," in *Black Theology: A Documentary History, vol. 1, 1966–1979*, ed. James H. Cone and Gayraud S. Wilmore (Maryknoll, N.Y.: Orbis Books, 1993), pp. 27–36.

11. See "Womanist Theology," in *Black Theology: A Documentary History, vol. 2, 1980–1992*, pp. 257–351.

12. See Victor Anderson, *Beyond Ontological Blackness: An Essay on African-American Religious and Cultural Criticism* (New York: Continuum, 1995).

13. See "The Second Generation," in *Black Theology: A Documentary History, vol. 2, 1980–1992*, pp. 15–75; see also Josiah U. Young, *A Pan-African Theology: Providence and the Legacies of the Ancestors* (Trenton, N.J.: Africa World Press, 1992); Dwight N. Hopkins and George Cummings, eds., *Cut Loose Your Stammering Tongue: Black Theology in the Slave Narratives* (Maryknoll, N.Y.: Orbis Books, 1991); Dwight N. Hopkins, *Shoes That Fit Our Feet: Sources for a Constructive Black Theology* (Maryknoll, N.Y.: Orbis Books, 1993); Garth Kasimu Baker-Fletcher, *Xodus: An African American Male Journey* (Minneapolis: Fortress Press, 1996); Riggins R. Earl, *Dark Symbols, Obscure Signs: God, Self, and Community in the Slave Mind* (Maryknoll, N.Y.: Orbis Books, 1993).

14. See Anthony B. Pinn, *Why, Lord?: Suffering and Evil in Black Theology* (New York: Continuum, 1995). Pinn is building on an earlier critique of black theology by William R. Jones, *Is God a White Racist?: A Preamble to Black Theology* (1973; reprint, Boston: Beacon Press, 1998).

15. See "New Directions in Black Biblical Interpretation," in *Black Theology: A Documentary History, vol. 2, 1980–1992*, pp. 177–254; Cain H. Felder, *Troubling Biblical Waters: Race, Class, and Family* (Maryknoll, N.Y.: Orbis Books, 1989) and his edited work *Stony the Road We Trod: African-American Biblical Interpretation* (Minneapolis: Fortress Press, 1991); Brian K. Blount, *Go Preach!: Mark's Kingdom Message and the Black Church Today* (Maryknoll, N.Y.: Orbis Books, 1998); Theophus H. Smith, *Conjuring Culture: Biblical Formations of Black America* (New York: Oxford University Press, 1994).

16. W. E. B. Du Bois, *The Souls of Black Folk* (1903; reprint, Greenwich, Conn.: Fawcett, 1961), p. 23.

17. Martin Luther King, Jr., "Beyond Vietnam," a pamphlet of the Clergy and Laymen Concerned About Vietnam, April 4, 1967.

18. *The Souls of Black Folk*, p. 23.

Whose Earth Is It, Anyway?

The second epigraph is cited in Samuel Rayan, "The Earth Is the Lord's," in *Eco-theology: Voices from South and North*, ed. David G. Hallman (Geneva: WCC, 1994), p. 142.

1. See *Justice, Peace, and the Integrity of Creation*, papers and Bible studies edited by James W. van Hoeven for the World Alliance of Reformed Churches Assembly, Seoul, Korea, August 1989; and Preman Niles, *Resisting the Threats to Life: Covenanting for Justice, Peace, and the Integrity of Creation* (Geneva: WCC, 1989).

2. See Delores Williams, "A Womanist Perspective on Sin," in *A Troubling in My Soul: Womanist Perspectives on Evil and Suffering*, ed. Emilie M. Townes (Maryknoll, N.Y.: Orbis Books, 1993), pp. 145–147; and her "Sin, Nature, and Black Women's Bodies," in *Ecofeminism and the Sacred*, ed. Carol J. Adams (New York: Continuum, 1993), pp. 24–29; Emilie Townes, *In a Blaze of Glory: Womanist Spirituality as Social Witness* (Nashville, Tenn.: Abingdon Press, 1995), p. 55; and Karen Baker-Fletcher, *Sisters of Dust, Sisters of Spirit: Womanist Wordings on God and Creation* (Minneapolis: Fortress Press, 1998), p. 93.

3. Robert Bullard, *Dumping in Dixie: Race, Class, and Environmental Quality* (Boulder, Colo.: Westview Press, 1990), p. 31.

4. Cited in Bunyan Bryant & Paul Mohai, eds., *Race and the Incidence of Environmental Hazards: A Time for Discourse* (Boulder: Westview Press, 1992), p. 2. See also "African American Denominational Leaders Pledge their Support to the Struggle Against Environmental Racism," *The A.M.E. Christian Recorder*, May 18, 1998, pp. 8, 11.

5. Cited in Robert D. Bullard, ed., *Unequal Protection: Environmental Justice and Communities of Color* (San Francisco: Sierra Club Books, 1994), p. 20.

6. Benjamin Chavis is now known as Benjamin Chavis Muhammad and is currently serving as the National Minister in Louis Farrakhan's Nation of Islam.

7. Bunyan Bryant, "Introduction" to his edited work *Environmental Justice: Issues, Policies, and Solutions* (Washington, D.C.: Island Press, 1995), p. 5. Benjamin Chavis defined environmental racism as "racial discrimination in environmental policymaking. It is racial discrimination in the enforcement of regulations and

laws. It is racial discrimination in the deliberate targeting of communities of color for toxic waste disposal and the siting of polluting industries. It is racial discrimination in the official sanctioning of the life-threatening presence of poisons and pollutants in communities of color. And, it is racial discrimination in the history of excluding people of color from the mainstream environmental groups, decisionmaking boards, commissions, and regulatory bodies" ("Foreword," in *Confronting Environmental Racism: Voices from the Grassroots*, ed. Robert Bullard [Boston: South End Press, 1993], p. 3).

8. *National Black Church Environmental and Economic Justice Summit*, Washington, D.C., December 1–2, 1993, The National Council of Churches of Christ in the USA, Prophetic Justice Unit. This is a booklet with all the speeches of the meeting, including the one by Vice President Gore.

9. See Ronald A. Taylor, "Do Environmentalists Care About Poor People?" *U.S. News and World Report*, April 2, 1984, p. 51.

10. John Lewis's quotation is cited in Deeohn and David Hahn-Baker, "Environmentalists and Environmental Justice Policy," in *Environmental Justice: Issues, Policies, and Solutions*, p. 68.

11. Alice Walker, *Living by the Word: Selected Writings, 1973–1987* (San Diego: Harcourt Brace Jovanovich, 1988), p. 173.

12. "Do Environmentalists Care About Poor People?" p. 51.

13. Ibid.

14. Ibid.

15. Audre Lorde, *Sister Outsider* (Trumansburg, N.Y.: Crossing Press, 1984), p. 110.

16. Catherine Keller, *From a Broken Web: Separation, Sexism, Self* (Boston: Beacon Press, 1986), p. 5.

17. See Elie Wiesel, "Nobel Peace Prize Acceptance Speech," <http://home.sol.no/~solhanse/wiesel.htm>, December 10, 1986.

18. Cited in Leonado Boff, *Cry of the Earth, Cry of the Poor* (Maryknoll, N.Y.: Orbis Books, 1997), p. 2.

Credits

"Christianity and Black Power" from *Is Anybody Listening to Black America?* Edited by C. Eric Lincoln. Copyright © 1968 by The Seabury Press, Incorporated.

"Black Spirituals: A Theological Interpretation" from *Theology Today,* vol. 29.1 (April 1972).

"Black Theology on Revolution, Violence, and Reconciliation" from *Union Seminary Quarterly Review,* vol. 31.1 (Fall 1975).

"Black Theology and the Black Church: Where Do We Go from Here?" from *Cross Currents,* vol. 27.2 (Summer 1977).

"The Theology of Martin Luther King, Jr." from *Union Seminary Quarterly Review,* vol. 40.4 (1986).

"Martin Luther King, Jr., Black Theology—Black Church" from *Theology Today,* vol. 40.4 (January 1984).

"Martin Luther King, Jr., and the Third World" from *The Journal of American History,* vol. 74.2 (September 1987).

"Demystifying Martin and Malcolm" from *Theology Today,* vol. 51.1 (April 1994).

"New Roles in the Ministry: A Theological Appraisal" from *Black Theology: A Documentary History, 1966–1979.* Edited by Gayraud S. Wilmore and James H. Cone. Copyright © 1979 by Orbis Books.

"Black Theology and the Black College Student" from *Journal of Afro-American Issues,* vol. 4.3&4 (Summer/Fall 1976).

Acknowledgments

Many people made this book, like the others, possible. A special thanks is due to Mary Graves and Louise Wareham, my assistants. Their first-rate assistance enabled me to devote my time to teaching and writing. I should also mention Adam Clark and Sylvester Johnson, my research assistants, who were adept at finding every reference I requested and called to my attention many others in my field of interest. Sylvester also read the manuscript and assisted me in the selection and the organization of the essays and the index.

A thanks is also due to Judy Diers, friend and former student. She also read most of the manuscript and made important editorial suggestions.

Thanks to the Union Seminary community for their support of my work. During my three decades at Union Seminary, I have had many provocative and challenging dialogues with my faculty colleagues. I wish I could mention all my students—past and present—during my years of teaching at Union Seminary. They heard all these essays as lectures and challenged me to think deeply about the implications of my claims. Still, every time I begin a semester of teaching, it is like the first one—tremendously exciting and deeply challenging. Union students are special. They remind me daily of the awesome responsibility and great joy of teaching and writing.

I should also express a word of gratitude to the many colleges, universities, and seminaries and to the churches and communities around the world where I presented these lectures. Their support of my work is deeply appreciated.

I also want to thank my friend Deborah Chasman, Editorial Director of Beacon Press, for passing my manuscript on to Tisha Hooks, whose encouragement and editorial expertise were much needed. An author could not ask for more.

Index